CW00405227

F

The author

Tim Newell has thirty eight years' experience as a prison governor, retiring in 2002 from Grendon, the therapeutic establishment.

He has been a Quaker for seventeen years, active with Quakers in Criminal Justice and Aylesbury Quaker Meeting. He has helped with the development of Circles of Support and Accountability in England, with restorative justice developments in custodial settings and with the development of services to those traumatised through bereavement by murder and manslaughter, Escaping Victimhood.

Forgiving Justice

a Quaker vision for criminal justice

Tim Newell

Swarthmore Lecture 2000

Revised edition 2007

QUAKERbooks

First published May 2000, revised edition April 2007

Quaker Books, Friends House, 173 Euston Road, London NW1 2BJ

www.quaker.org.uk

ISBN 978 0 901689 51 1

Cover design Hoop Associates

Cover image detail from the painting 'Searching' by Tom Carrigan, who used to be a prisoner at Grendon

Book design and typesetting Golden Cockerel Press Ltd, London, based on original design by Jonathan Sargent

Copy editing John Banks; revised edition, Deborah Padfield

The Swarthmore Lecture

The Swarthmore Lectureship was established by the Woodbrooke Extension Committee at a meeting held 9 December 1907: the minute of the Committee providing for an "annual lecture on some subject relating to the message and work of the Society of Friends". The name Swarthmore was chosen in memory of the home of Margaret Fox, which was always open to the earnest seeker after Truth, and from which loving words of sympathy and substantial material help were sent to fellow workers.

The Lectureship continues to be under the care of Woodbrooke Quaker Study Centre trustees, and is a significant part of the education work undertaken at and from Woodbrooke.

The lectureship has a twofold purpose: first, to interpret to the members of the Society of Friends their message and mission; and second, to bring before the public the spirit, aims and fundamental principles of Friends. The lecturers alone are responsible for any opinions expressed.

The lectureship provides both for the publication of a book and for the delivery of a lecture, the latter usually at the time of Britain Yearly Meeting of the Society of Friends. A lecture related to the present book was delivered at Yearly Meeting in London on the evening of 27 May 2000.

The Swarthmore Lecture Committee can be contacted via the Clerk, c/o Woodbrooke Quaker Study Centre, 1046 Bristol Road, Selly Oak, Birmingham B29 6LJ.

Woodbrooke
Quaker Study Centre

Contents

An overview   9

Acknowledgements   13

1 Still searching   15

2 Why Quakers are interested in criminal justice   20

3 Criminal justice today: a historical perspective   34

4 Restorative justice and community safety   50

5 Restorative and community justice working   61

6 Theology, justice and forgiveness   75

7 Quaker social testimony   88

8 Organisational and cultural change   91

9 Working with cultural change   100

10 Ideas in action   107

11 Proposals for a way forward   119

12 Towards a Quaker vision of community justice   129

Appendix 1: Circles of Support and Accountability   137

Appendix 2: Ideas for group study   142

Appendix 3: Ideas for practical work   153

Key issues in the development of prisons in England   160
and Wales to 2007

Glossary of terms   167

Reading I have found helpful   176

An overview

In Chapter 1, I present my personal credentials, beliefs and assumptions as I approach the subject of criminal justice. My experience of working within the Prison Service of England and Wales led me to continue to explore the potential within the prison whilst deeply aware of the limitations. Prison should be used as a sanction of absolute last resort.

In describing *Why Quakers are interested in criminal justice* our changing experience through many roles over 350 years is significant. The varied thinking behind the function and purpose of punishment and imprisonment as described by Quakers reflects thinking about a just society. The contrast between earlier designing of prison regimes and current resistance towards the dependence on custody as the predominant solution to problems of crime shows the response to such issues from an informed and involved faith community. Some issues for future attention are presented towards the end of the chapter describing the concept of restorative justice – a key focus for current and future thinking and action.

Criminal justice today provides an outline of current issues, tracing the development of recent issues and changes within systems. I describe the effects of imprisonment and contrast their lack of effectiveness in achieving the purposes ascribed to them by public expectation with the potential of imaginative community-based alternative approaches. The potential of uniting the prison and probation services into one National Offender Management Service is considered. The growth of local partnerships of statutory agencies such as the police and probation services with voluntary groups and faith communities provides an optimism that is attracting increasing support.

Restorative justice and community safety outlines the nature of some of the work developed through restorative principles of considering the needs of the victim as central to the purposes of criminal justice. The experience of partnerships of voluntary and statutory agencies working together to provide safer communities has been a source of inspiration to many and I describe the work of one such group with a look at the potential for the future.

Restorative and community justice working provides some examples of family group conferences, victim/offender groups and a study over several years of a community partnership approach in Ludlow, which was described at Yearly Meeting 1999.

Theology, justice and forgiveness describes fundamental considerations of spiritual dimensions which underpin the justice systems and which reflect our beliefs in the nature of being human. The spiritual processes behind the stages of committing a crime, admitting guilt, feeling repentant, offering reparation, seeking forgiveness and reconciliation depend upon recognising the importance of the potential within each person. I emphasise the significance of forgiveness in considering why the spiritual process stops often at an admission of guilt with little else expected from the person. Using the procedures of restorative justice can lead towards an opportunity for the full experience of feelings of making reparation and moving towards forgiveness to take place as part of a natural process of communication within a process of valuing and respecting the people involved, victim and offender.

Quaker social testimony describes how our testimonies are applied within the criminal justice process. This leads us naturally to work with the ideas of restorative justice, emphasising community safety and resisting the recourse to imprisonment except in very limited circumstances. The development of a more inclusive approach towards resolving community conflict is part of our vision.

In order to consider ways of applying our vision and converting faith into action, I propose a model of possible change in *Organisational and cultural change*. The emphasis changes as systems behind an organisation are described through the detailed consideration of the dynamics involved. I consider the paradigm or mindset behind the criminal justice system and describe the resistance to change with suggestions about how change could be approached. Understanding the complexity of the deep-seated beliefs behind the criminal justice system, such as the supporting myths and stories, can lead to an awareness of how change can be considered.

Aspects of this paradigm are further considered in *Working with the cultural change*. Myths and stories behind the justice system are examined in proposing the possibility of change. If we understand

and challenge such myths at a fundamental level a strategic shift may well be possible, to reflect the values of an inclusive approach towards justice.

I illustrate *Ideas in action* by giving accounts of meetings between victims and offenders. Through this process victims can be seen to have benefited by taking more control over how they perceive the traumatic episode of the offence. The offender begins to learn the truth about the effect their behaviour has on another person's life. The meeting is an opportunity to say sorry and to begin to accept that and to move towards forgiveness.

Proposals for a way forward considers practical involvement in issues and opportunities to lead to a culture shift over time. I describe the international perspective in an agenda for change that will address most of the major issues of current concern, and our experience of applying faith in action through Circles of Support and Accountability.

Drawing from examples of our experience through opportunities, *A Quaker vision of criminal justice* describes our approach to community justice combining a vision of the current value and the potential in each person with a challenge to the institutions which do not uphold this vision.

Throughout the work I have referred to offenders and prisoners in the masculine. I am aware of the high incidence of women in custody and the need for particular attention to be given to the effects of their detention on them and their families. Female prisoners accounted for six per cent of the prison population of England and Wales in 2005, although the number of women in custody has more than doubled over the past ten years. What I have said about prisoners and offenders refers to all groups with their many different identities and needs.

I am conscious that in writing about the criminal justice system I have not referred to my experience of governing. This is in an attempt partly to make what I say accessible to a wider readership and also not to limit my ideas purely to the prison setting. I am full of enthusiasm for the place in which I used to work, Grendon Prison. The values of truth, trust and consent are intrinsically woven into the daily activity of caring for the most difficult prisoners, who are seeking to carry out the most demanding of experiences – personal change – through learning about self in community with others. My commitment to working with dangerous people in creative ways has been confirmed by my ten years of governing Grendon – but that is another story.

Tim Newell

Acknowledgements

I have been greatly helped in working through issues to write this work.

Pam Lunn and Elisabeth Salisbury of the Swarthmore Lecture Committee have been stimulating, supporting and understanding throughout the period of thought and preparation. The balance between acceptance and challenge has been critical in working through the issues.

Being a member of Aylesbury Preparative Meeting has been a source of inspiration, calm and immense support. John Mitchell, a member of the meeting, has challenged me through many of the legal aspects of my thinking.

Being a trustee of the Alternatives to Violence Project (AVP) has given me access to the inquiring mind of Kimmett Edgar, whose wisdom helped me through the strategic issues. His continuing support in working through the implications of trying to be restorative in a punitive setting has been vital.

My contact with Victim Support has enabled me to benefit from the wider perspective and awareness of Barbara Pensom.

Through my membership of the Crime and Community Justice Group at Friends House I have been closely supported in gaining a deeper awareness of restorative justice processes by Marian Liebmann. Mike Nellis and Martina Weitsch have assisted by their clear thinking and vision.

I have been fortunate to be included in the Parliamentary Dialogue group that has worked with Michael Bartlet, who has brought an awareness of the legal and political implications to my thinking.

Through my working environment of the Prison Service I have been greatly helped by William Payne, who succeeded me as Governor at Grendon, by Jim Gomersall, who was Deputy Governor at Grendon Prison where I worked, and by Giles Charrington, who has been my coach and counsellor for the past ten years. Much of my early thinking of this work was helped by Professor David Wilson, a past prison governor and now a teacher and communicator on criminal justice matters. Working closely with Robert Davies, then Assistant Chief Constable of Thames Valley Police and Malcolm

Bryant, retired Chief Probation Officer of Berkshire, has also been stimulating and helpful in seeing the wider picture.

My sister, Janet Newell, has provided clear comment about balance and detail as only a family member can.

Without the willing acceptance of my wife Ann I could not have attempted to start on this part of my journey.

Second edition

In revising the work of seven years ago I have been greatly affected by my experience as a restorative justice facilitator with the Justice Research Consortium's research project in the Thames Valley and I am indebted to Geoff Emerson for his understanding of my beginnings in the work. I have also been privileged as a trustee of Old Jordans to establish some creative work with victims of crime and for that I thank Val McFarlane, Barbara Tudor and all the facilitators who have risked themselves in creative, challenging ways.

Thanks to the following for use of their material:
Community Reintegration Project, Robert Davies, Hampshire & Thames Valley Circles of Support & Accountability, Marian Liebmann, Mediation UK, Lesley Moreland, Lorraine Nolan, Margaret Smith and *Thame Gazette*, Jamie Wrench.

Chapter 1
Still Searching

I was a Governor in the prison service from 1965 to 2002 and
have been a Quaker for the past sixteen years. The possible
incompatibility of those two experiences has been drawn to my
attention on several occasions, and I felt it most acutely when I
read *Six Quakers Look at Crime and Punishment* (1979). The strong
suggestion that punishment is contrary to our peace testimony
caused me serious searching, as did the occasions when I have had
to order force to be used particularly in situations of hostage taking,
cell barricades or settings of serious disruption to the life of the
prisons I have governed. How was I able to reconcile my position
as a Quaker and remain part of an organisation whose primary
function is still to detain people against their will?

I strongly believe in the presence of God in every person and
particularly in every prisoner. The damage that some people have
done to others through their dangerous behaviour justifies some
setting in which they can be detained to consider the effects of
their actions and to seek some other way of behaving. If this could
be done within the community through strong relationships of
supervision and oversight, duly authorised, then there would
not be a need for prisons; but such enlightened arrangements
do not at present exist. Without them society requires a coercive
containment for some to be held safely and understand the effect
of their behaviour on others. This containment should be kept to a
minimum necessary for victims and communities to feel safe and
restored through the process of protection.

If it were possible to realise such a possibility in the community
then I could foresee the end of prisons, but at present there is no
psychological acceptance that offenders remain the responsibility
of their communities, and there is still a strong belief that people
learn from being hurt. There are undoubtedly people who need to be
held in security for the sakes of themselves and others. But we must
take care how we identify them and their dangerousness hence the
debate about the detention of those dangerous people with severe
personality disorder. This brings into focus the ethical dilemma of

balancing the safety of the community against the rights of a person who has not committed an offence. I am concerned about the dependence upon prisons for holding the disturbed, as the rationale for so doing is reliance upon the belief that they deserve such punishment and that it will eventually lead to their improvement and to the safety of their communities.

Why prisons?

The idea of basing the justification of imprisonment on the harm that has been committed leads me to question which harms justify the deprivation of liberty. Murder and rape clearly do. Probably burglary but not theft because of the effect on the person (burglary is often an invasion of someone's home as well removal of goods from it), but this is debatable if it implies that property is more important than people are. Other reasons for imposing sentences of imprisonment, such as offences arising from drug dependency, benefits fraud or driving offences, define crimes which are unlikely to be clearly harmful in a way that would justify imprisonment. Other crimes that do not usually lead to imprisonment – such as environmental crimes of deliberate pollution – could be said to be more generally harmful than many burglaries. The justification for imprisonment is often based on the need not only to establish and communicate boundaries of acceptable behaviour for us all but also to enable the offender to have time for the possibility of reparation and restorative opportunities.

I have seen my work in prisons in the context of providing a place of safety for all in custodial communities. My mission has been to try to help those detained to accept their behaviour and to learn about the consequences of it upon others in order that they can return home safer people, able to make a citizen's contribution to society. If the setting has been less than ideal for this process, I have worked to ameliorate the damaging aspects of imprisonment. The development and maintenance of prisons where there are relationships of respect and care both between staff and prisoners and between prisoners and prisoners have been a demanding experience.

It is through the provision of positive activity of a stimulating and relevant sort that learning about the self can take place. I have been particularly attracted to the vision of Ann Wetherall, who saw the potential of each prison cell as an ashram or place of spiritual learning and development. From her vision and the work of the Prison Phoenix Trust hundreds of prisoners have been helped and continue to be supported through seeing their time in prison as an opportunity for personal growth. The connection between prisons and spirituality has been clear to me ever since I cycled with 'borstal boys' to church services at the start of my work in the Prison Service. As the son of a borstal chaplain I worked with 'borstal boys' on our vegetable garden, long before I joined the Service. My studies of monastic life in visiting historic sites showed me that calling prisoners' and monks' accommodation 'cells', says much about the Victorian ethic behind imprisonment. We too saw the prison, like the monastery, as a place for penitence, and Americans called it a penitentiary.

I have been very conscious of victims throughout my work. This awareness is particularly clear for primary victims, those who are made by the damaging behaviour of offenders, some of whom are related to them and many of who are their neighbours. I have met victims and have been present at meetings between the person who offended against them, and have mediated some understanding and forgiveness. I have been the victim of crime and have been helped by meeting the person who broke into my house. I have helped many offenders who have been victimised while in custody to understand the nature of their experience and to begin to make connections with others similarly distressed. The focus of much of my work has been with the families of offenders, from the days when I worked with the parents of young men distressed and humiliated by their family being stigmatised, to grieving with those whose loved ones had killed themselves in prison. The connection I have been able to make with families has been greatly helped by my own family's support for me in my work and by their active participation in the relationships within the prison institutions in which I have worked.

I have been sustained in my commitment to work in prisons by strands of personal relationships and also by my belief that there is a need to detain those who have been damaging to others and are likely to remain so unless held. The growth of publicly expressed punitive attitudes and the political rhetoric of toughness have tested my capacity to continue, but I have always considered that my presence within the organisation has better enabled me to affect the conditions of many prisoners and staff than if I were to leave and criticise from outside. Throughout this conscientious engagement I have often wondered if the last order received is really a step too far, but I have always been able to reconcile action with a pragmatism that is founded upon a consistent optimism about human nature and the regular experience of shared fellowship with staff and prisoners.

My awareness of the dynamics of institutional life has made me conscious that the critical relationships in the prison are those between prison officers and prisoners. It is here that the experience of loss of freedom can be experienced with some respect and dignity. Thus my concentration as a governor has been upon supporting the opportunities for creative and enabling relationships, to make it safe for people to care for each other in a sometimes stark and cruel setting. I have been surprised by the mutual level of concern that is shown within relationships of control.

Prisons work?

Despite this enthusiasm for working at the small steps of improvement in conditions and the development of caring relationships I have always maintained that prisons should be places of last resort – that they should not be seen or promoted as places for transformation and change even though I know they can become that for many. If we can possibly treat people in the community near their homes, with their families to support them and share in the change necessary to avoid being more damaging, then we should do that. Prison does not work – in reconciling communities. It is, however, a necessary evil in the current state of our sense of community and given our inability to sustain an inclusive approach towards those who offend against us and who are offensive. Unless we can feel safe as a society, we will continue to need places of last resort where we can place those who are perceived to be dangerous to us. The fact that we resort to prison too quickly is a reflection not of crime rates but of our degree of inability to tolerate and embrace the 'other' in our society, those who are different, difficult and require too much effort on our part to include them in our social intercourse. Prison has to work for now, but I hope to reduce its need and to reduce its damaging effects on 'souls in pain'. I continue to search for way to work to those ends.

Chapter 2
Why Quakers are interested in criminal justice

Two slogans from the early 1970s convey the flavour of the special relationship Quakerism has with the state:

If you want peace, work for justice.
Question authority.

One of the core functions of the state is to regulate the use of force, against those perceived to be enemies of the state, both from without and from within. Quaker pacifism inevitably fosters a critical perspective on the use of force by the state.

In the seventeenth century, Quaker theology developed a unique understanding of the state. The first generation of Friends experienced the power of government brought to bear on them as though they were enemies. However, early Friends did not engage in counter-attacks or foment revolution. They recognised the power for good in government while remaining fearless in offering criticism where they felt it was due. Quakers based their beliefs and actions on individual conscience, and refused to view the state as an absolute, as the ultimate arbiter of good and evil.

Where some other religious groups took the view that the world was inherently evil and shunned community life, Friends desired to live in the world as we find it. Thus Friends recognised a duty to scrutinise the workings of the criminal justice as the use of force by government against its own citizenry.

At some periods of our history, the faith in human goodness has threatened to eclipse a more realistic caution about our capacity to do harm to each other. But Friends are pragmatic. We believe in human goodness, but we also lock our houses when we go out for the evening. Friends show a similar sense of balance when working with those in authority. The people who make decisions about the use of force against our fellow citizens are only human, and their efforts need to be supported with constructive criticism.

These moral balances – between the individual and the state; between human goodness and our capacity to do harm – colour our vision of how force is used for social control. For example, one of the traditional aims of imprisonment has been rehabilitation. In the early nineteenth century, there was tremendous faith that science could provide the solution to criminality; that criminals could be reformed. At the opposite pole, the 'nothing works' philosophy of the early 1980s denied that programmes intended to change offenders resulted in reduced rates of reoffending. On an individual level the key question is whether one can change.

Quakers' beliefs lead to diverse ideas about rehabilitation. On one hand, Friends believe that people have the potential to change. This faith in the goodness of the individual led American Friends to advocate the 'silent system', which was intended – in retrospect a misguided intent – to help the criminal to listen to the inner voice of conscience. The 'silent system' involved a prohibition on any verbal communication between prisoners and staff and between prisoners and prisoners, which led to large numbers of prisoners developing severe mental health problems. On the other hand, Friends questioned the justice of having someone in authority determine how long one spends in prison according to their judgement of whether or nor the prisoner is fully rehabilitated.

Friends are not always conscious of and in tune with the history of the Quaker relationship to the criminal justice system. We know that we have a reputation for prison reform but not how or why. Thus an important part of our history and formative experience has become lost in our consciousness, and it was John Howard who worked closely with Friends in his campaigns to raise the consciousness of the public, who wrote of prisoners that no 'criminality of theirs justifies our neglect'. However, through our history, through our experience as prisoners, penal reformers and designers, as practitioners and as campaigners for human rights, we have a legacy which we are still searching to come to terms with as we face the current unprecedented growth of the system.

Friends have experienced prison from both sides of the bars. This gives us unique insights into an important social institution. We are aware that criminal justice is an area of social activity which reflects the values of a society most clearly and which has the strongest impact on the most vulnerable groups.

As prisoners

The early persecution of Friends and the imprisonment of George Fox (1624–1692) clearly brought home to the developing Society the reality of being locked up. Early Quaker meetings were primarily concerned to receive reports of those who were suffering, so that they and their families could be looked after. The continuing experience of being outsiders led to a deep awareness of the psychology of and sympathy for the excluded within the Society's learning and culture.

'What a hurtful thing it was that the prisoners would lie so long in gaol, showing how that they learned badness one of another in talking of their bad deeds, and thereby speedy justice should be done.' George Fox's words in his *Journal* foreshadowed three principles of modern penology: early trial, the classification of prisoners and the provision of work.

Quakers have been ready to take the consequences of their principled stands that have often taken them outside the law. The spirit in which Friends have suffered the experience of prison, particularly in the seventeenth century, is also special in that Friends seemed to accept prison cheerfully, as a response to their civil disobedience. In more recent times the experience particularly of wartime conscientious objectors led to a heightened awareness of conditions within prisons for many. This led then to action to challenge conditions and the all too ready recourse to custody. Stephen Hobhouse was one whose work following his experience as a conscientious objector led him to describe in great detail the destructive experience of imprisonment. The price that objectors paid during the war of 1914 and the courage they showed were not lost, for during the 1939–1945 war most objectors were recognised as men under obedience. Recent campaigners for green issues and anti-nuclear protesters have faced imprisonment, which again has led to an experience of the role of prisoner. Their experience shines as a beacon for the Society to learn from and celebrate.

Quakers are represented among the generality of prisoners. Several prisoners have become Quakers during their sentence and find their way through the experience of imprisonment and the ministry of Quaker Prison Ministers and other Friends.

As reformers

The 'Great Experiment' of William Penn (1644–1718) in the governance of Pennsylvania in the 1670s, in which he abolished capital punishment for all crimes except murder, showed the earliest example of Quaker thought converted into action. He made a home for the protection of Friends and guaranteed freedom of worship, as well as treating the indigenous people in the territory with respect. He laid down that 'prisons shall be workhouses', that bail should be allowed for minor offences, and 'all prisons shall be free, as to fees, food and lodgings'.

Penn's followers were 'credited' with the invention of the penitentiary, (the idea of the use of containment as a beneficial and transforming experience) and there are examples of many Friends involved in establishing what was considered a more just treatment of offenders. Although it has been pointed out that they were only a minority within this establishing movement in the Pennsylvanian reform groups, nevertheless these American Friends' voices were clearly highly influential in asserting the morality of the new concepts. The idea was a completely new one: that imprisonment should be looked on as a means of reforming criminals and not merely punishing them.

John Bellers (1654–1725) was the earliest British Friend to pay serious and systematic attention to social reform. He pleaded for the abolition of the death penalty, the first time this plea had been made. He argued that criminals were the creation of society itself and urged that when in prison there should be work for prisoners so that they might return to the world with an urge to industry. Bellers issued in 1724 an Epistle to Friends, pleading for a combined effort at penal reform, but there was no response. The ideas had come too soon. Only in Pennsylvania did the ideas find a place in the eighteenth century, serving as an example which was later to modify the penal code throughout the United States.

In eighteenth century Britain the concept of imprisonment in itself as a sentence was influenced strongly by the Christian notion of spiritual revival. John Howard's important work *State of the Prisons* (1777) drawing attention to the conditions of prisons was strongly supported by Friends who developed the Society for the Improvement of Prison Discipline and the Reformation of Juvenile Offenders. They

23

supported Howard's promotion of an Act of Parliament in 1774, which although enacted sadly did not lead to the desired changes, because public opinion was not ready to make it work.

Elizabeth Fry (1780–1845) was the most famous of Quaker reformers but there were others equally influential at the time of the formation of ideas about the nature of prison regimes, and later for the promotion of some regime components. Elements of prison life such as the separation of women and children from men and the development of purposeful activity of work or education, came about through the example and pressure of informed people. Elizabeth Fry's work in Newgate raised public awareness of the horrors of the women's prison. She gave evidence before a Committee of the House of Commons revealing the facts she had unearthed and outlining the principles of reform that would remedy the worst of the corrupt practices. Although she never saw the results of her work in raising the awareness of those in power, her work remains an inspiration to those who understand the courage called for in taking on this cause.

Among other Quakers who maintained the impetus towards penal reform were William Tallach, Marjory Fry and Roy Calvert. William Tallach, Secretary of the Howard League from its inception in 1866 to 1879, became a leading influence against the death penalty. Marjory Fry (1874–1958), as Secretary to the Howard League in 1921 and later as a researcher and writer, challenged the emphasis on punishment of the offender with little consideration being given to the effect of the offence. This led eventually to the Criminal Injuries Compensation Board (1964) and indirectly to legislation leading to compensation orders. Roy Calvert (1898–1933) was a leading reformer against the death penalty and raised the public awareness to the background of the issue.

David Wills (1903–1980) was a centrally important figure in the development of what is regarded as being one of the most just and humane types of holding regime. In the 1930s he developed the concept of therapeutic communities in the Barns in Peebles for boys aged nine to fourteen, based on principles of relationships and self-learning. His was a strong influence at Glebe House in Cambridgeshire, which was set up in 1969 and is still continuing as a therapeutic community for teenage men. His understanding of punishment as intrinsically evil brought him to lead the Society to take up the issue – *Six Quakers look at Crime and Punishment* published in 1979, was the result. The ideas contained in the book were not universally accepted but it provoked much thought and discussion. The idea that punishment in itself is contrary to the fundamental principle of God's purpose continues to challenge those who work within the criminal justice system.

As designers

The design of institutions is very important in determining what happens within the structure and how people relate to the environment in which they find themselves, and how they relate to each other. Architecture, particularly in buildings designed to constrain and control, can predetermine what regime can operate. The serried rows and tiers of cells reinforce the anonymity of prisoners. The contrast of the diminutive individual beside the almost monolithic scale of prison buildings also reinforces the subjugation of the individual.

The design of prisons and their regimes was influenced by Friends following the work of Jeremy Bentham (1791), who aimed to regulate individuals and their relationships so as to minimise harm and suffering overall. They also followed the development of prison architecture in Pennsylvania during the late eighteenth century to reflect concepts of the spiritual possibilities of custody. The panopticon design of a prison as a place in which all activity could be seen, so that the individual was continually aware of the presence of authority, came from such concepts. The design was not adopted, however, as it did not reflect the practical aspects of prison management of large numbers of people. The building of Pentonville in 1842 in a radial design as a model prison put other ideas of control into action in England and the success of the design persisted through the most active time of British prison building in the nineteenth century.

The 'separate' and 'silent' systems were founded in the early nineteenth century on the principle that imprisonment was a time for solitary introspection and ascetic, spiritual self-improvement. American Friends supported these ideas: they were brought to England where they were developed as prison regimes and became the focus of attention during the mid nineteenth century. The idea of separate and silent confinement seems to have emerged almost by accident. First, John Howard observed, in his *State of the Prisons* (1777), that prisoners were being housed with each other with no control over their association. He expressed concern about experienced criminals passing on criminal values like a plague. His phrase 'seminaries of vice', borrowed from Fielding, captured the anxieties of policy-makers on both sides of the Atlantic. Secondly, reformers in Philadelphia read Howard as an inspiration. One of the first reforms they made to the Walnut Street Jail (1790) was to separate the men from the women. Impressed by the order and control this gave them, they designed the first penitentiaries – Western and Cherry Hill (1820) – to accommodate prisoners in individual cells. They theorised that isolation would prevent the spread of criminal values, and it would also encourage introspection and repentance. Hence Cherry Hill began to practise separate confinement, while Auburn (New York State) practised co-operative workshops run in silence in the 1850s. The 'separate and silent' system then returned to England through enthusiasts. John Howard was horrified. He wrote to Jeremy Bentham that he never intended such a system. He explained that he meant no more than that prisoners should have separate quarters for sleeping at night. He feared that total separation would lead a man to madness, which was what it did in increasing numbers. This eventually led to a relaxation of the systems in England and Wales by the 1880s.

Other Quaker influences on the development of prison regimes include the work of William Tuke who in 1792 developed the concept of the asylum as a separate place for the mentally ill, in the Retreat in York. This helped the cause of removing such people from prison settings. In setting up the Retreat he ensured that the treatment of mentally ill reflected their dignity as people, in sharp contrast to the severe treatment which prevailed elsewhere.

American Friends were central in the development of the idea of parole in the 1960s and the indeterminate sentence at a stage when the treatment potential of prison regimes was thought to be effective. But by the 1990s they had become strongly opposed to the same ideas as unjust when concepts of 'just deserts' became more prevalent. (This argument was based on the concept that justice can best be served by clear links between the offence and the punitive consequence. Ideas about treatment in custody as a reason for detaining people were thought to be unfair.) They argued that the dignity of the offender would be best served by another approach towards sentencing. The view that 'nothing works' in the treatment of offenders led to this 'struggle for justice' movement, which asserted that indeterminacy of sentence was unjust because people could serve long sentences for very minor offences, if their underlying behaviour had shown cause for concern.

Struggle for Justice – the primary American Friends' text in opposition to rehabilitative sentencing – was published in 1972. It proposed that authorities held too much power over prisoners under treatment. The authors argued against the power of parole authorities to hold someone in prison longer for what they might do rather than for their offence. (Their thoughts are echoed in our current deliberations over the British government's proposals to detain those with anti-social personality disorders, whose behaviour is considered potentially dangerous.) However, the outcome of their campaign was that others pressed for the 'just deserts' approach, resulting in longer periods of imprisonment and mandatory minimum sentences. (History could repeat itself with the current debate, as the alternative to reviewable sentences for those with severe personality disorders appears to be longer and longer determinate ones.)

Many Quakers are now at the forefront of the movement to provide alternatives to imprisonment. For the past twenty years, some Friends have been at the forefront of developing the concepts of restorative justice.

As commentators

There is a strong Quaker tradition of writing about criminal justice issues, and yet there is little agreement on policy issues that unites Friends in developing a testimony on the subject. There has not been a Swarthmore Lecture on the subject until now despite obvious concern since the start of the Society. There have been Lectures concerned with wider justice issues – in particular the ideas behind what I refer to as restorative justice were outlined in John Lampen's *Mending Hurts* (1987).

The Penal Affairs Committee and British Friends decided in 1968 that the time had come to challenge the Society's assumption that, as long as reforms were pursued as in the past, imprisonment was acceptable. In 1970 *Why prison? A Quaker View of Imprisonment and Some Alternatives* was published, urging Friends to consider fundamentals rather than simply mitigating the more superficial faults of the system. The victim was to be considered more centrally but only as part of the reform of prisons and their slow abolition. In *Six Quakers Look at Crime and Punishment* (1979) David Wills and others set out to show that punishment is inconsistent with our peace testimony and that we should work at all levels to create a 'non-punitive society'. There was no general acceptance of the practicality of working towards this ideal within the Society after its publication or in 1985 when the subject was looked at again. Both the compilers of *Quaker Faith and Practice* (1995) and many Quakers have expressed disappointment at that publication's failure to draw together a view about criminal justice 'because Friends are still searching for a corporate view'.

Mike Nellis's Rowntree Fellowship experience in 1997 renewed the search for a testimony about 'community justice'. In his travels and writings he has awoken the concerns of many groups and of the Society at the centre in establishing further thought and action on the subject of revitalising penal reform. He developed the important concept of *community justice*. He linked community safety (the political goal of the current administration), with restorative justice (a challenge to the adversarial system and the possible scapegoating it causes) and hostility to custody (a concern of Quakers for much of the past three decades). This composite view of the complexity of the interrelatedness of ideas and issues can lead us to a greater awareness and eventually a more effective capacity to act. The emphasis upon local action from community justice groups through restorative justice approaches could have a major impact within the Society. It could channel our concern into effective local initiatives which are already being driven through but which would benefit greatly from our spiritual perspective. It is this combination of faith and action which has great possibilities for us and which can be seen through respected examples of development.

The setting up of a Crime and Community Justice Committee

in 1997 builds on the emerging wish in the Society to seek a common view. This group seriously considers the ideas of community justice, with its emphasis on the opportunities afforded by the developing interest in restorative justice in action. The committee also reviews the work of communities establishing local crime prevention strategies and Youth Justice Panels following the Crime and Disorder Act of 1998. A call for Friends to become involved at local level in such initiatives reflects the work of Mike Nellis in establishing local Crime and Community Justice groups within several Monthly Meetings.

As workers

Historically, many Quakers have worked within the criminal justice system, both as sentencers and as practitioners within the Crown Prosecution, Police, Prison and Probation Services. It is this crucial experience which forms the basis of our emerging testimony. There are many Quaker magistrates and members of Independent Monitoring Boards of prisons. Their insight into the dynamic of balancing the needs of the individual offender, the victim and the community that they serve is invaluable in reaching a realistic and workable approach towards justice. The Probation Service has been particularly attractive to Friends, and there have been a few who have worked in the Prison Service, including Duncan Fairn who became a prison commissioner, and who was a Swarthmore lecturer. Others have included Dermot Grubb, governor of Oxford and Bristol Prisons in the 1970s.

The pioneering work of Bob Johnson in C Wing Parkhurst during the 1990s has left many unanswered questions for the criminal justice system, particularly those concerned with the treatment of offenders with severe personality disorders. There was evidence during Bob Johnson's work with some of the most disturbed and dangerous men in our prisons that through his ways of treating them there were marked changes in their behaviour and their approach to themselves and others. The close work with the early life experiences of damaged people, reaching to their 'terror and rage' and enabling them to speak about the unthinkable, showed remarkable results both in the lives of individuals in the unit but also in the general ambience of C Wing. The level of emergency alarms dropped dramatically, as did the use of medication and incidents of self-harm and of violence. Much of the therapeutic interchange material was recorded on video and there would be good opportunities for research to test out the long-term effectiveness of the work, if the Prison Service would only engage with Bob Johnson rather than resist and seek to have the tapes confiscated and destroyed. With the increased interest in anything which appears to work with severe personality disordered offenders after the failures of treatment methods in special hospitals, particularly Ashworth (where the latest scandal involving patients being out of control led to a major review of the special hospitals), there is an opportunity to learn from one of the few success stories in this troubled field. Arising from his work, Bob and Sue Johnson have formed the James Nayler Trust, which is dedicated to exploring the healing work with dangerous offenders and those affected by mental illness, using the concepts of 'Truth, Trust and Consent'.

The establishment of Quakers in Criminal Justice in 1987 arose from the need to provide a focus and support for those working and connected with the justice process. This important network continues to provide the Society with a reservoir of skilled and informed members. Penal Affairs Committee was laid down because it was felt that its narrow remit did not permit the consideration of the wider issues relating to criminal justice and that these could be pursued through other organisations, many of whom represented views close to those of Friends.

The work of Jan Arriens in founding Lifelines has enabled a greater awareness for many through daily contact with the horrific limitations of the policies and practices behind the death penalty. It has provided for those on Death Row in the United States to be in touch through correspondence with concerned members of society. The human spirit has hope even in the most soulless situations.

The Alternatives to Violence Project (AVP) developed in the 1980s in United States prisons as a response from Friends to a request from prisoners for support in addressing the level of violence within prisons in New York. This has led to a worldwide movement providing workshops in the community and in prisons. In Britain in 1990 AVP started working with support from Friends House, but then in 1997 became an independent organisation.

The experiential workshops run in prisons represent the hope that people can transform their capacity to handle situations that in the past would have resulted in violence. Workshops last for three days and involve participatory exercises leading to the development of a sense of confidence in each person to begin to manage their violence in a more socially acceptable way. The sense of community which workshops develop is an important experience of hope for increasing numbers of prisoners. LEAP Confronting Conflict (based in London) has provided similar structured experience, particularly for young offenders, with much success.

Under the auspices of Friends World Committee for Consultation, Quakers have been attending the United Nations' Congresses for the Treatment of Offenders and the Prevention of Crime for the past twenty-five years. At the Congress in 1990 in Cuba, a resolution on life imprisonment was passed, based on the study by Nick McGeorge, published that year by the Quaker Council for European Affairs. A United Nations report on life imprisonment, requested by that resolution, was prepared by Sean Eratt, a Quaker intern working in the UN offices in Vienna. He was funded jointly by QPS and QSRE. Translated into Arabic, French and Spanish, it has been one of the best received reports from the UN Criminal Justice Division.

Another report from QCEA, this time on crowd control, resulted in Quakers being involved in the drafting of the UN Code on the Use of Firearms by Law Enforcement Officers. Since 1991 the main decision-making body on criminal justice issues at the UN has been the Commission on Criminal Justice and Crime Prevention. Quaker representatives have been attending the annual meetings in Vienna. The focus of Quaker concerns are the continuing use of the death penalty, the weakening of human rights in criminal justice systems, the heightening of interest in restorative justice and the growing incarceration of women with its serious implications for wider groups in society.

Since 2000 Quakers, through Quaker Peace & Social Witness have been at the forefront of developing work on Circles of Support and Accountability, providing community involvement for high risk, high need sex offenders released from prison. Through trained volunteers meeting weekly with the 'core member' there have been

31

some remarkable experiences of sustained community experience for ex-offenders who are usually outcast within their settings. Working in partnership with statutory agencies, this work has been respected at all levels and has shown the way to counter fear and hatred, being an example of faith in action, respecting that of God in all people.

There are many Quakers working in the criminal justice system, and particularly in prisons, whose contributions may be unsung but are no less valuable for that. The volunteers who come in through the Chaplaincy, the presence of Quaker prison ministers (QPMs) and the holding of Meetings for Worship in many places can make telling contributions to the lives of individuals and to the institution.

As resisters?

There is a tradition amongst Friends for active resistance to developments that are against our testimonies – the opposition to nuclear weapons for instance. The continued construction of prisons, particularly with the current emphasis on their building and running by the private sector, has been the focus of some concern but as yet no direct action by Friends. However, it is a subject for direct challenge that remains a possibility as we seek the way ahead. Friends are active in Amnesty International and have been active in the campaign against imprisoning asylum seekers. The developing work of Turning the Tide provides training and support for those working at issues which call for a challenge to the established way of arranging matters. The leadership of Quakers in witnessing for peace is well described in the 2005 Swarthmore Lecture *No Extraordinary Power* by Helen Steven.

Increasingly we see evidence of a reliance on force rather than human community to ensure safety. Theories of defensible space have led to a rapid expansion in private security, gated communities, intruder alarms and barbed wire fences. The 'fortress society' is one in which those with the means barricade themselves away. Yet, whether on an international or an interpersonal scale, force does not demonstrably reduce risk or conflict.

The problem will not be fixed by better equipment, more ruthless means of defence or greater restrictions on the people who are considered a threat. Technical details such as these disguise the fundamental issue that gives rise to the sense of threat. The reactions to the horrific events of 9/11 show that hitting out and using force leads to a greater sense of injustice and resistance. Respectful dialogue leading to understanding must be the eventual way ahead if we are to avoid greater fear.

If you want peace, work for justice.

The uncertainty and sense of danger is not caused by some external threat, but is a result of injustice. The problem is divisiveness driving out community, and force destroying the opportunity to build lasting trust.

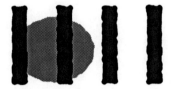

Chapter 3
Criminal justice today
A historical perspective

The debate about the causes and consequences of human behaviour in the context of offending is constantly with us. The decision whether someone is 'sad, mad or bad' is a complex one and can lead to significant differences in treatment within the criminal justice system. If 'sad' then the implication is that practical help is called for to remedy unfortunate circumstances. If 'mad' then there is a need for psychiatric treatment. If 'bad' then there is considered to be no excuse and therefore the individual deserves punishment and prison. Throughout the last two and a half centuries during which imprisonment has developed into the punishment we know today, society's approach to its use has variously reflected attitudes to prisoners as sad, mad or bad.

In Victorian times the prevalent economic *laissez faire* climate emphasised the individual's personal responsibility. Accordingly, the British system of justice was based on retribution ('just deserts') and deterrence. All were equal before the law and could expect equal punishment if they transgressed. The main penalty became imprisonment with the decline in transportation following the American War of Independence, although the thinking was the same: it was 'getting rid'. And just as transportation offered an opportunity for 'redemption' of a materialistic sort, so the silent and separate systems of imprisonment offered chances for 'redemption' of a moral sort – or so it was thought.

Changes towards reformation and rehabilitation (albeit through a quasi-medical model of 'treatment and training') were initiated by Parliament at the beginning of the twentieth century. They established the Probation Service, juvenile courts and borstals and new penal institutions that emphasised reformative and educative elements. The use of probation introduced the concept of alternatives to imprisonment, particularly for first- or second-time offenders. The sentence began to be tailored to the individual rather than to the crime. People were seen as individuals to be pitied, cared for and if possible reclaimed. Thus reform was the central aim.

The expert became more significant and individual responsibility became less stressed. This led to greater humanity in treatment but also to a more patronising approach towards offenders that led sometimes to long sentences for trivial crimes in order to achieve reform.

The demise of 'treatment and training' occurred in the 1970s following some research that seemed to indicate that 'nothing works'. The fact that this research was to some extent flawed in its approach did not stop the momentum towards abandoning many of the positive elements of regimes that had been developed over the years. Ironically this was taking place at a time when the social sciences were growing to new influence. The absence of a belief in a positive, reformatory purpose of imprisonment led to the development of such unlovely concepts as 'humane containment', in which a rehabilitative concept was absent.

The purposes of imprisonment can be explored from different perspectives as we consider the future of prisons. These purposes have been described as having a social function on behalf of the community, having a function within the criminal justice system and having their own objectives as institutions. Thomas Mathieson (1965), who sees the following elements involved in imprisonment, has described the function on behalf of society:

- *expurgatory function* – those who are disruptive and unproductive are contained so that they can do little damage
- *power-draining function* – those detained in prison cannot interfere with the normal processes of production and are also unable to exercise any responsibility as prisoners
- *symbolic function* – those on the outside can distance themselves from people who are publicly labelled as prisoners
- *action function* – people are reassured that something is being done about the problem of law and order, and
- *diverting function* – while attention is focused upon the sort of offences which the lower working class commit it is diverted from the serious social harm caused by companies and corporate crime.

Within the criminal justice system the prison's function can be described as:

- *custodial* – keeping under control those detained for the purposes of the court or as a result of the sentence of the court
- *coercive* – persuading fine defaulters who will be released on payment
- *punitive* – serving the sentence of the court.

The function of the institution has altered considerably over the recent past. During the height of confidence in rehabilitation in 1964, Prison Rule No. 1 stated, 'The purpose of the training and treatment of convicted prisoners shall be to encourage and assist them to lead a good and useful life.'

However, during the 1970s there was a decline in such certainty epitomised by the research of Martinson (1974), who described the effect of many regimes in prisons when writing 'Nothing, or almost nothing works'. Concepts of 'humane containment' were proposed to try to reduce the likelihood of continuing to use imprisonment for what were still perceived as positive reasons. The May Committee (1979) reporting on the Prison Service put forward the idea of 'positive custody' with elements of keeping prisoners in secure yet positive ways, preserving and promoting self-respect and preparing them for their discharge from prison. Neither 'humane containment' nor 'positive custody' was taken up.

By 1983 the Prison Service had a statement of tasks: 'to provide as full a life as possible consistent with the facts of custody and help prisoners keep in touch with the community'. This retreat from the high ideals of changing human beings was reflected in the 1988 'mission statement',

> Her Majesty's Prison Service serves the public by keeping in custody those committed by the courts. Our duty is to look after them with humanity and help them lead law abiding and useful lives in custody and after release.

Sadly, conditions in prisons were deteriorating, with overcrowding, an increase in the number of escapes, a lack of facilities for work and education and the number of assaults by prisoners on staff and other prisoners. The Home Office in 1990 referred to the danger of prison being an 'expensive way of making bad people worse'.

The objectives of criminal justice policy established in the 1980s were developed within a framework of evidence and principle. The evidence was growing about the nature and extent of crime, the characteristics of criminality and patterns of criminal careers, methods of preventing crime and criminality, the effectiveness of sentencing, the integrity and effectiveness of policing and the management of prisons. There were disturbing factors within Prisons, Probation and Police Services which led to a search for identity. The Financial Management Initiative from the government sought increased effectiveness and value for money. By 1985 this led to a set of objectives for the criminal justice process that included the following:

- to prevent and reduce crime
- to establish a principled basis for sentencing
- to avoid the unnecessary use of imprisonment and stabilise the current prison population
- to develop supervision schemes in the community to reduce reoffending
- to give greater consideration to victims and
- to make the system more efficient, effective and accountable.

Principles arising from these objectives included proportionality in sentencing (some consistency in length and severity), due process and accountability in administration, including accessible channels for complaint and respect for individuals, including members of ethnic or cultural minorities. They included also an empirical or evidence-based approach to the formulation of policy and the development of operational policy. Thus the sentencing principles behind legislation were made explicit in recognising the limited effect of custody except for those who really needed to be kept from the public because of their dangerousness.

The Crisis of Control

There was some evidence of a reduction of the use of the criminal justice process with the development of an increasing awareness of the negative consequences that follow exposure to the formal apparatus, particularly the courts and prison. Experience and practice led and shaped policy, particularly when there was collaboration across agency boundaries. Nevertheless, sentences were increasing in length over the 1980s. Greater severity for violent offenders coinciding with a reduction in severity for others was promoted as a 'twin track' approach that found expression in the Criminal Justice Act 1991. The Act was very clear that imprisonment should be the last resort in sentencing. Although this was attractive in seeking to discriminate between the serious offender and those less dangerous to society, there was a danger that the more punitive aspect of sentencing could be stressed, as did happen after 1992, when the length of sentences increased.

Events of 1990 at Strangeways Prison and later at several others when prisoners rioted were the subject of an inquiry by Lord Justice Woolf. I was governing Winchester Prison at the time of the disturbances and sadly there was a small episode within that prison with a few prisoners breaking through onto the roof. The psychological disruption caused by the Strangeways precedent and the fact that the incident there was allowed to last for over 25 days changed the nature of relationships in all prisons for some time. The confidence of staff and prisoners in being able to sustain safe co-operative working together had been badly affected. The disturbances, which spread anxiety to all prisons, came at a time when improvements were being introduced into prisons, with more out-of-cell activity and better regimes. However the overcrowded conditions and the limited response from the Service to matters of individual care and justice resulted in a great outpouring of resentment and anger.

Lord Woolf's report *Custody, Care and Justice* is the most fundamental and considered analysis of the dynamics of prison life. The recommendations and what we have learned from the report are still to be fully acted upon, and they provide a visionary agenda for the future of custody. Issues of balancing the dynamics of custody, care and justice were dealt with in an imaginative yet realistic manner. The concept of a 'contract' for each prisoner, which set out rights and responsibilities, was proposed, with the setting of a limit for each prison's population. The key concept of the community prison, with prisoners held close to their community for most of their sentence, remains an ideal that is still being sought. Although the White Paper which followed it and the Criminal Justice Act 1991 acted on several strands of Lord Woolf's recommendations, the fragility of political consensus soon became apparent, with serious consequences, as we shall see.

The Woolf Report made recommendations about the physical conditions within prisons that were significant in ensuring reasonable living and working environments, for example the abolition of the inhumane practice of 'slopping out'. It made clear comments about the regimes and the principles which should underlie the treatment of prisoners, including justice, care and responsibility. The report commented on the large numbers of mentally disordered offenders in custody and recommended that diversionary strategies should be supported. The isolation of the Prison Service from other agencies within the criminal justice process was to be remedied by the establishment of a Central Criminal Justice Co-ordination Committee and local area (commonly called Woolf) committees to establish a forum in which systems of justice could be more integrated.

Within the Probation Services there were significant changes. Between the 1930s and the 1960s the 'diagnostic ideal' held sway in the concepts behind the treatment of offenders. The main arguments used had been based on moral and religious concepts of mercy and the promise of reform. However, with the growth of the ideas behind psychoanalysis becoming more widely adopted as the rationale behind probation treatment, the expertise of probation officers became accentuated, with offenders now regarded as 'clients'. In the 1970s however with the challenge to the effectiveness of any form of treatment – 'nothing works' – there was a crisis within the probation approach. A more managerial approach had developed as the service had grown. Attempts to continue treatment approaches were developed with the growth of the 'What Works' movement in the early 1990s, focusing on offence-specific work as well as targeting and disciplining the process of such interventions. Significant changes in direction were brought about as the government sought to use probation as a form of control and punishment and to use probation officers as managers of programmes carried out by the voluntary sector.

A change of political direction occurred at the end of 1992 that can be summarised as leading towards an approach to social issues and criminal justice in particular based more on exclusion. Principles emphasising personal freedom and individual responsibility and a disregard for the influence of situations and circumstances epitomised the dominance of a deserving majority. Members of this self-reliant, law-abiding group are entitled to benefit themselves and are contrasted with an undeserving, feckless, welfare-dependent and often dangerous minority or underclass from whom they need to be protected. The new public managerialism that emerged at this time supported this approach with its contractual and market-based ideology. The emphasis was upon the delivery of services with maximum efficiency, effectiveness and, often above all, economy. The contrast between high-trust and low-trust approaches to the management of organisations is clearly seen in this development and in the move towards a closer regulation of risk management, which led social work agencies to become more cautious. There was a move towards greater 'safety' in public organisations, with the state perceived as doing the minimum for the social order to be maintained.

This change in direction was accompanied by rhetoric which encouraged the use of imprisonment and which led to an unprecedented rise in the prison population. In turn this caused extreme pressures on a system already disrupted by the concerns for security arising out of two major escapes and the subsequent inquiries which resulted in massive expenditure on security measures. Added to these pressures were the continuing constraint of budgetary reductions and the threat of market testing as private sector companies demonstrated that they could run prisons more economically owing to their lower unit costs for staff. Many of my colleague governors became quite depressed over this time as they began to dismantle some of the regimes which they had been used to painstakingly building over the past few years.

The disillusionment of the Prison Service was matched by the lowering of morale in the Probation Service, whose identity was constantly under examination during this period. The particular focus on the change in emphasis of the training from an approach based on social work towards greater control and management caused the most concern.

Current developments, although more hopeful in some ways, continue to place an emphasis on the rhetoric of toughness and control. However, the dynamics of the 1998 Crime and Disorder Act, in ensuring that local communities will develop their own initiatives to tackle crime within the locality, must lead to a greater ownership of the problem by local people and therefore more involvement in seeking solutions. We shall look in more detail at restorative justice and community safety in chapters 4 and 5.

The continuing development of legislation concerned with criminal justice over the past seven years has moved thinking on towards a greater focus on effectiveness in meeting targets set by the Government in response to public concerns. This change can be seen in the summary below.

Summary of the key changes

The Prison Service has faced massive change over the past fifteen years.

1990   Discarding all that went with Rule One's 'a good and useful life' for 'humane containment' was the mood at the start of the period.

1991   There was a period of 'renewed optimism' with the Woolf Report and the period of Joe Pilling as Director General.

1993   With a greater move towards managerialism under Derek Lewis and the emphasis on 'incapacitation and general deterrence' of Michael Howard the Service shifted to regimes intended to be 'decent but austere' under increased pressure of numbers because 'Prison Works'.

1994   Under-enforcement of rules led to high profile escapes, then the Woodcock and Learmont Reports and the sacking of Derek Lewis.

1995   Richard Tilt, Director General developed managerial approaches with an emphasis on security. The Service has since become safer for the public, prisoners and staff.

1999   Martin Narey, Director General introduced tighter managerial controls with an emphasis on 'decency and effective delivery'.

2003   Phil Wheatley, Director General, has sustained the need for effective delivery within the context of moves to integrate the prison and probation services under the National Offender Management Service.

2006   National Offender Management Service (NOMS) established to combine Prison and Probation Services in delivering a seamless sentence and experience for offenders designed to meet their real needs in reducing reoffending.

Changes of approach in prison life

The inner life of prisons within which staff have to operate has changed rapidly in the period with resultant confusion. The emphasis has shifted from

- Justice and Humanity (1990–93) through
- Redisciplining Austerity (1993–97) to
- New Effectiveness plus (1999–2007)

Prison staff have been asked to respond in the way they manage prisoners and prisons according to the political emphasis of the day. Is there any wonder there is confusion and conflict within their relationships at all levels?

Part of the flux and uncertainty arises because few of the concepts have been grounded on ethical values and beliefs. There may be a much greater emphasis on this aspect within the role of prisons as the wider concept of sentencing impact becomes clearer. Prisons will need to pursue values of justice, tolerance, decency, humanity and civility as they establish their legitimacy with prisoners, the wider NOMS setting and the community.

A framework to look at values in approaches to crime may be helpful. This is derived from the work of Andrew Rutherford.

STRATEGY A Punishment	STRATEGY B Efficiency	STRATEGY C Care
Moral condemnation	Pragmatism	Liberal humanitarian
Dislike of offenders	Management, systems based	Empathy with offenders
Degradation	Smooth administration	Optimistic, inclusive
Unfettered discipline	Process oriented	Belief in constructive work
Expressive function of sanctions	Lack of correctional ideology	Open and accountable processes
	Separation of action from belief or sentiment	Links with social policy

Strategy C dominated 1990–93 with reinforcement from the Woolf Report and Joe Pilling's Back to Basics speech of 1991 combined with the Criminal Justice Act of that year.

From 1993 Strategy A dominated thinking under Michael Howard's Home Secretaryship – combined with a developing Strategy B particularly after the escapes in 1994.

From 1997 Strategy B has dominated with subtle managerial and political changes which suggest a fourth strategy.

STRATEGY D
Effectiveness

Standards for all aspects of work

Protection of public a key ideology

Regimes and programmes subject to accreditation

Reducing offending a key outcome

Best value from resources

Links with other agencies to maximise effectiveness

Pressures on prison staff to operate within these concepts are based on the following assumptions:

- There is an identifiable criminal class – people who are dangerous or a nuisance who can be distinguished from law-abiding citizens and from whom law abiding citizens must be protected (100,000 people are estimated as being responsible for the majority of crime).
- People who offend do so as a result of rational choice, from which they can be deterred if the chances of being found out are high enough and the consequences are sufficiently severe.
- Interventions can be effective in preventing reoffending.
- Public confidence requires 'tough' sentences.

We might like to challenge these assumptions with the following criticisms:

- From a human rights perspective the policy is criminalising children

43

- Net widening effect stigmatises more people as criminals
- Disabling and socially divisive effects of the policies
- Compromising civil liberties
- Risking more miscarriages of justice

There is a challenge to the assumption that there should be a separation between sentencers and the impact of their sentences is contained in the purposes of sentencing as outlined in the Criminal Justice Act 2003.

- Punishment of offenders
- Reduction of crime
- Reform of offenders
- Protection of the public
- Reparation (to the victim or the community)

Two other challenges are present as significant movements which may well affect prison staff

- Restorative Justice, through which it is expected that the offender should do something to repair the damage they have caused and if possible achieve some reconciliation with the victim. This concept is slowly being accepted by the Government and a strategy is in place to introduce it through NOMS, possibly into prisons where it has been tried out and found to be effective.

- Responsible Sentencing says the court, NOMS and the offender all have responsibility for deciding what should be done with the sentence, for what they should between them try to achieve and for bringing about that result.

Staff roles will change in the face of these likely changes as restorative approaches spread to all aspects of prison life – complaints, adjudications, anti-bullying policies etc. Responsible sentencing will involve staff being more involved in decision making and sentence planning decisions and delivery. These prospects are hopefully more ethically based than previous initiatives.

Continuing concerns

Within all these developments remains a lingering concern that the aims of imprisonment are not achievable because of the irrationality of the system.

It has not been possible to demonstrate conclusively the possibility of *rehabilitation* through custody – indeed we have seen through empirical studies that the opposite is clearly the case for most prisoners. The prisoner's social system seems to enable the prisoner to reject any internalising of the rejection he is experiencing and instead reject his rejecters. People are damaged by the experience of imprisonment. They are subject to several additional risks while in custody, such as to their life and health through increased victimisation (from living in a close community of sometimes difficult and dangerous people), susceptibility to disease especially those following HIV infection and Hepatitis B and exacerbated risk of suicide and self-harm. Other risks include being vulnerable to arbitrary treatment by prison staff who exercise power at all levels, and the risk to their social well-being through a reduction in their employment and earning capacity. Additional risks are the likelihood of strained family relations and lost housing and the probability of returning to prison having been increased through the demoralising experience of incarceration.

Individual deterrence rarely works in scaring away the person brought into custody: the prisoner subculture works strongly against this. The evidence is that reconviction rates, particularly among young people who have been in custody, are high – for those over twenty-one the reconviction rate after two years at risk is 65 per cent, for those under twenty-one it is about 80 per cent. There is limited evidence from the work carried out by programmes targeted at offenders that the rate of reconviction can be reduced. Although some reduction can be achieved by focusing on those in prison, the real improvement and original criteria for success of much of the cognitive behavioural work contained in the 'What Works' syllabus is dependent on community-based work. The evidence is that, where there is a good grounding in the locality in which the offender lives and remains after the intervention is concluded, the results are even more impressive.

It is difficult to show that there is a *general deterrence* by the system on those who have not come into contact with it, but the evidence is that the effect may be very slight. The probability of detection shows some effects but the severity of the punishment appears to have little effect. The preventive inefficiency of prison constitutes a communication problem in that the intent to prevent further offending is not working. The rise in reported rates of offending continues. Punishment is a way in which the state tries to communicate a message to society about the unacceptability of certain anti-social behaviour. It is a crude form of communication and yet continues to be pursued.

Incapacitation of large groups of offenders in order to ensure they are not able to continue to commit crime is largely the policy in the United States. It is not effective either when done routinely or when done selectively. The estimates of increased incarceration that would be necessary to deliver effective incapacitation have caused even the most tough-minded to reconsider this approach. The figures indicate that to reduce crime by 1 per cent in England and Wales the prison population would have to be increased by 25 per cent (Tarling, 1993). Although there is a clear understanding that dangerous individuals can be restricted from committing offences while held in custody such restriction does not significantly reduce the number of other potentially dangerous people in society. However, the emotional security which is generated by such feelings of knowing that a dangerous person is behind bars can lead to a feeling of safety for many. This does not lead us to accept incapacitation as a realistic option, whether for logistical, economic or moral reasons.

Lastly there is the *retributive* element which suggests that the criminal offence can be balanced by time in prison. The elements of a crime and its sanction are so variable that they cannot be established as in balance, and the punishment scale gives little satisfaction to the victim. From the evidence of successive British Crime Surveys, victims seek the detection of offenders and think that they should primarily put right what went wrong – through reparation, through an act of apology and often an explanation of their behaviour.

We know from research and expressed opinion that the experience of imprisonment is one of psychological deprivation.

Sadly, the person regularly imprisoned somehow adapts to the environment and the experience of deprivation which takes place in custody.

The loss of *liberty* can be painful for people used to determining their own choices and movement as the constraints of custody are all too evident given the emphasis on security and control that dominates prisons. Unsupervised movement is severely limited. Because of the constraints prisoners will either check every movement out with staff and so become very dependent upon them or will deny themselves any uncertainty by limiting their involvement in activities.

The deprivation of *autonomy* within a custodial setting dominates the daily routine in which the individual has to sacrifice personal wishes in order for the whole institution to function. Thus the timing of daily events is often governed by the staffing, and with the reduction of resources in prisons some aspects of this control of routine have been increased. Men have spoken to me about the considerable length of time it takes to grow out of the routine of having meals early in the day, lunch at 11.45 and the main meal at 16.45, once they are released.

The stripping of the person coming into prison has been well described by prisoners, and particularly their feelings of personal assault have affected their perception of the whole experience. The *loss of goods and services* upon which we place so much of the expression of our personal identity can be very painful because of the significance of the possessions in the lives of those constrained. Some of the most stressful situations in prisons have occurred when there has been a change in the level of goods prisoners are allowed to have in their possession. I once had a disturbance in a prison to handle because I introduced a restriction in the number of personal pictures men were allowed to have in their possession and display in their cell, even though this had been introduced with long discussion and explanation.

The *loss of heterosexual relationships* while in custody can affect self-perception for many prisoners and can particularly exaggerate the macho culture within the prison. Many often have difficulty in expressing their tender side, and this can give rise temporarily to homosexual relationships in an attempt to do this. It is only in settings of trust as in Grendon that I have experienced the joy of real belly laughter with prisoners and the extreme distress of bereavement, normally such feelings are subdued in order to survive the lack of trust in the air.

Despite the control of the setting, the experience of most prisoners is one of *a loss of personal security.* Given the nature of the population, it is likely that there will be much uncertainty about the colleagues with whom one is sharing this experience. The high prevalence of mental disorder in prison as shown by recent research by the Office of National Statistics, which has indicated that over 60 per cent of the prison population has a serious personality disorder, clearly makes for great instability within the prison community. The predominant feeling many prisoners will speak about is fear.

The way that people adjust to the deprivations of the prison experience is to establish rules and cultural norms that enable some certainty to be maintained at least for most of those in custody. This creation of a set of expectations will be formed by the predominant culture of the group that is delinquent, anti-authority and dependent upon force. There are many who cannot take part in this culture, and often they become the casualties of prisons – those who are mentally disordered have limited recourse to treatment although increasingly this is becoming available; those who are depressed can be made worse by the experience and we know that the incidence of suicide in prison is some ten times that in the community; those who have strong ethnic minority attachments may have problems in being accepted within this predominantly white, male environment. Thus there are several groups who could be unable to participate in the predominant culture within a prison and who may therefore find it hard to make sense of the time in custody or to use it to their advantage.

If people became aware of how poorly prison as well as other parts of the criminal justice system really protected them, there might well be more concern about our emphasis upon them. If they also knew that people coming out of prison are sometimes more dangerous than they were coming in, there might well be a wish to reduce their use. People are rational, unlike prisons. The emphasis upon evidence-based policies, what has been shown through research to work, in criminal justice practice is a sign of hope that movement will be towards establishing the purposes of decisions and towards finding more rational approaches to sentencing.

Chapter 4
Restorative justice and community safety

It is partly because those working within criminal justice systems have lived with an understanding of the flawed system that the ideas behind alternative systems of justice are beginning to become more attractive to practitioners and sentencers. The concepts behind restorative justice with its emphasis on the victim are central to any consideration of providing a safer society. Restorative justice recognises that offenders have a part to play in helping the victim and the community feel safe again. This is achieved when offenders accept their responsibility for the offence without the criminal justice process and thus seek to make voluntary reparation. Restorative justice ideas have been likened to a cuckoo in the nest of the criminal justice system, and indeed the concepts are a challenge to the traditional adversarial system of establishing guilt.

The relationship between legal concepts of guilt and restorative justice are controversial but family group conferencing (one example of restorative justice principles in action in which those affected by the crime meet together to establish the truth and seek resolution to restore harmony within the social setting) acknowledges the offender's legal guilt and works from there to design a means of reparation. Where restorative justice stands in starkest contrast to the criminal justice system is in the retributive function. Whilst restorative justice can accommodate a finding of guilt, it would oppose any response that is punitive for the sake of punishment alone. It will always be necessary to have a formal system in which due process is at work in order to test the evidence against those who do not admit their part in an offence. This system could be informed by research into the effectiveness of sentencing and a development of 'What Works' principles. The system could also be more directed towards finding out the truth about what happened in a particular event or series of events surrounding a crime rather than being focused upon the behaviour and person of the accused. In developing a restorative approach to carrying out adjudications on disciplinary matters in prison I have been impressed by how readily prison officers and prisoners have taken to the opportunity to talk through the issue of conflict between them within a setting in which all are going to have a say in the outcome.

In comparing and contrasting restorative justice with traditional criminal justice, concern has been expressed that the focus in restorative approaches on reparation can deflect attention from the offender's guilt. Hence the metaphor of a cuckoo in the nest gives the image of a subversive revolution. It may be preferable to consider the mutually complementary dimensions of the two responses to crime. The criminal justice process is mainly defined by a legal code (laws) and by the punitive consequences of law-breaking. Thus its primary aim must be to establish beyond doubt that the accused person is guilty and deserving of the sanction. In contrast, restorative justice is based on society's acknowledgement of the damage that results from crime. The aim of restorative justice is to clarify how the crime has harmed people (including, but not limited to, the victim and the offender) and to find ways to repair that harm. Put simply, then, criminal justice is about laws, guilt and sanctions; restorative justice is about emotional, physical, material harms and what can be done to make amends for them. In this sense, the two approaches are complementary and can help to address the damage that some people have done to others through their dangerous behaviour. Such a complementary understanding of traditional criminal justice and restorative justice would challenge us to find ways of combining the two in response to every crime, rather than offer two separate roads as choices.

Community safety is a developing concern under current legislation and there is increasing experience of agencies working together in partnership to support local community safety. The emphasis on developing strategies to prevent crime focus on environmental and structural factors rather than on detecting those who have broken the law. Thus the design of public places to make them safer through defensible space, good lighting and oversight has been shown to have an effect on local breakdown of safety. The practice of agencies which co-ordinate such work has proved very valuable in enabling the boundaries between such groups to be crossed in order to apply resources, skills and energy to solving problems with communities. There are increasing signs that criminal justice agencies such as the Crown Prosecution, the Police and the Probation and Prison Services have come together in certain areas to address issues of common concern. With the Crown Prosecution, Probation and Police Services now having the same geographical boundaries there can be more benefits in due course. The Prison Service will move to these boundaries under NOMS. This potential for transforming the practice of agencies in response to the real needs of communities will be our continuing concern during this work.

Restorative Justice

The assumptions behind restorative work are

- Repair – the main direction is to repair the harm caused by crime.
- Stakeholder participation – to involve those closely involved in a conflict in seeking to resolve it.
- Transformation in community and government roles and relationships – communities take over from agencies who help them come to justice through facilitative arrangements.

Applying these assumptions in a custodial setting calls for sensitivity and courage. There are several ways in which it has been applied, from fully restorative programmes such as conferences, through partly restorative ones such as community work projects and resettlement work to mostly restorative work such as victim/ offender mediation or therapeutic communities.

Restorative justice is based on the premise that the appropriate response to a crime requires much more than the delivery of a 'just measure of pain' to individual offenders, which appears to have been the basis for much policy till lately. Restorative justice is more concerned with the preservation and restoration of relationships both at an individual level and at a community level. It is not concerned just with healing the harm that has resulted from specific offences, important though that is. It is also rightly concerned with the prevention of future offending by addressing the factors that contribute to offending behaviour; and again these need to be addressed at both an individual and a community level. Thus the most important contribution that restorative justice has to offer is in the development of a broader social crime prevention strategy. Most other sentences of the court (and imprisonment in particular) tend to 'outlaw' or remove rather than integrate offenders; and actually can aggravate rather than reconcile the victim.

Restorative justice views crime primarily as injury (rather than law-breaking) and the purpose of justice as healing (rather than as punishment alone). It emphasises the accountability of offenders to make amends for their actions and focuses on providing assistance and services to victims. Its objective is the successful reintegration of both victim and offender as productive members of safe communities.

Procedurally, restorative programmes value active participation of victims, offenders and communities, often through direct encounters to identify the injustice done, the harm that resulted, the steps that are needed to make things right and actions that can reduce the likelihood of future offences. Programmes identified with restorative justice can be roughly divided into two categories: those that provide restorative processes, and those that provide restorative outcomes. Examples of the former include victim/offender mediation and reconciliation, family group conferences, victim/offender panels, sentencing circles and community crime prevention. I give accounts of these activities in Chapter 5. Examples of restorative outcomes include restitution, community service, victim support service, victim compensation programmes, rehabilitation programmes for offenders and so on. These are being more fully developed through the current strategies of the criminal justice agencies in partnership with the voluntary ones. A fully restorative system would be characterised by both restorative processes and outcomes.

Restorative justice has its critics. Some are concerned with the inefficiency of incorporating such processes dependent on examining and improving relationships in the context of the criminal justice system. Others worry that informal processes will result in violations of due process (the right to equal protection of the law, the right to be protected from cruel, inhuman and degrading treatment or punishment, the right to be presumed innocent, the right to a fair trial and the right to assistance of counsel). There is concern, that in urbanised and socially divided settings, communities are not likely to be able to play the role that restorative justice anticipates. Given the current momentum of the processes, these criticisms are likely to influence *how* restorative justice is incorporated into conventional criminal justice responses rather than *whether* they are incorporated.

Diversion at the caution stage is the most widely used in England and Wales, and was pioneered by the Thames Valley Police. This caution is at the earliest possible stage of action by the criminal justice system once offenders have admitted their behaviour. Some good experience has been gained, the work has been researched and there are indications of successful process experience (that participants feel better about the whole experience than through traditional procedures) as well as promising outcomes in terms of reconviction rates. Under the 2003 Criminal Justice Act, more widespread use of this cautioning process is taking place.

Diversion after charge is the process in which judges give authority in continental systems for the procedure to be dealt with through restorative principles. In common law traditions this power continues to rest in the prosecutor and thus it could be used more frequently.

Diversion after conviction involves cases that might be referred to a group conference or mediation/reconciliation programme. Another way would be to have a delay for participation in a restorative process as is common in the United States.

Mediation after sentence involves work between victims and offenders. At this stage such work can be very enriching for both parties, where there are no legal consequences. Certainly for victims it is clear that the motivation of the offender cannot be to 'get off' but to reach some understanding and look towards the future.

The role of the victim is central in restorative justice. The involvement of the victim by being informed and being involved in the process should be considered at all stages. There should be clear protocols in place which ensure that this is achieved with agreement and that there is no repetition of victimising the individual.

Community safety, criminal justice and partnerships

The new millennium has brought in astonishing new opportunities for improving the way we tackle crime and deal with offenders.

There is a climate of welcoming initiatives that reflect the potential for change in the person which is exciting and yet full of responsibility for those who have a chance to develop work that has not been possible for many years. The work of the Thames Valley Partnership, which has been operating now for twenty years, will be seen as highly relevant in helping to shape the agenda and take it forward. This optimism is based on the welcome development of a more inclusive social policy, the content and application of recent legislation and the emergence of three themes that can be seen at work across both criminal justice and community safety developments. These themes have been conceptualised as the three Rs of dealing with crime, Risk, Relationships and Reparation. They have the potential to become the foundations of a more integrated strategy for managing and reducing crime.

Risk

Managing and reducing risk of crime has been a central plank in crime prevention for many years. Measures such as closed-circuit television schemes, improved design of consumer products such as cars and a general increase in public awareness have all been enhanced through partnership initiatives. However, the disabling fear that ruins lifestyles and feeds off itself remains for some, and there needs to be a more realistic concern about crime to motivate people to take care of themselves, their neighbours and their possessions. Individuals must be helped in dealing with specific situations through a better use of information. The Probation and Prison Services are much more aware of the likelihood of reconviction of any particular group of offenders and yet recognise that whether a specific individual is one of those who will or will not reoffend requires a more complex assessment.

Relationships

Community safety and criminal justice have been influenced by the perception of crime as a breakdown in social relationships. This perception, coupled with the idea that everyone has a contribution to make to crime prevention, has underpinned the drive towards more effective partnerships. In addition the recognition of the poor service to victims in the past has motivated many to work to redress the perceived imbalance in criminal justice practice. The developing Thames Valley emphasis on restorative justice led in the autumn of 1998 to a joint statement by the Crown Prosecution, Police, Prison and Probation Services. This describes in practical terms what restorative justice principles will lead to in terms of actions. The CPS are giving greater emphasis to the needs of victims through better information and services for witnesses. The Prison Service has developed offending behaviour programmes with substantial victim empathy content, and the Probation Services will continue to develop their work with victims and the active support for victim support schemes.

The joint Thames Valley statement made it clear that 'Restorative Justice involves a more comprehensive and balanced view of crime. At its core is the concept of social inclusion, and the idea that individuals and the community as a whole have both needs and obligations.' It is, in short, about relationships which have been harmed and which need to be put right, rather than labelling and punishing for their own sakes. Perhaps not surprisingly the challenge which restorative justice represents to our traditional view of crime is experienced as particularly threatening by some lawyers who are specially wedded to the adversarial approach. We need to find ways to respond to their concerns without sacrificing the huge potential gains to victims and local communities which can be achieved through a continuing commitment to restorative justice. The overlap with partnership approaches to community safety is very apparent.

The Crime and Disorder Act 1998 represented a great opportunity for local authorities, the police and other agencies to establish new and better ways of working together. The creation of comprehensive local youth justice plans as well as specific innovations such as action plan orders and curfew and reparation orders are leading to a transformation of the way we deal with youth crime, and once again the community safety experience of partnerships is highly relevant.

Reparation

Reparation is a component of restorative justice and an important concept in its own right. At its core is the idea that the offender should wherever possible put right the damage done by crime by paying back something to the victim or the wider community. This has a widespread appeal to a sense of natural justice and the fact that it can be a positive constructive punishment that can benefit everyone.

This concept may well emerge as the most important issue over the next five years. The experience of Payback, a charity designed to stimulate awareness and acceptance of the advantages of community-based sentences, was a significant lead-up to the idea of reparation becoming central in the starting point for sentencing in future. The development of such a starting point will be through the thinking within the judiciary and the restorative justice agenda as well as the practical requirement to use community penalties which take pressure off the highest prison population in British history.

The community service order has had special benefits, and the arguments in favour of seeing community service as the normal starting point for determining sentences in most criminal cases rest on the special qualities of this unique method of dealing with offenders. Community service, now called community punishment, has great public and political support; it appeals strongly to a sense of natural justice; it involves a clear demand on offenders that they pay back the debt to victims and the community by working without pay; it contributes to the quality of life of local communities through the completion of a wide variety of useful work; it has consistently achieved excellent rates of successful completion and lower rates of reconviction; it costs less than prison and probation; and it is even capable of repeated use in selected cases. It contains something for everyone, and its potential should be recognised and developed. The discussion of the 'seamless sentence' promoted by successive Home Secretaries can clearly be based upon community service as the core element. The compliance of prisoners in open prisons with the requirements of community work regulations is remarkable. At the open prison in which I worked we released over 100 men a day to work in the community with charities, agencies, schools, homes and other projects. The results of good work transformed the perception of the public about offenders and changed the way that prisoners perceived community dynamics as well as their own capacity for good. This experience can now be part of a community sentence or of a custodial one, depending on the risk the person represents at the time.

There will be some cases in which the seriousness of the offence or the individual's personal circumstances precludes the community service order as a sensible or acceptable penalty. Those who are mentally disordered or heavily involved with drugs or alcohol, for example, may require special programmes. Such programmes will continue to be needed, and their development by probation and prison staff is to be applauded. The critical point is that it should be normal practice to start from community service as the presumed sentence and to argue away from it in exceptional cases rather than towards it, as is the case at present.

The profound changes in society that continue to stress personal responsibility and public accountability will lead to the increased use of community service as a sanction. Once again the link with the community safety agenda is clear. The identification of work projects which not only enable offenders to repay their debt but which also contribute to future community crime prevention is an exciting prospect. It is ultimately nothing less than the creation of a virtuous circle where real benefits can be gained from the original damage done by crime and future risk can be reduced.

The experience of restorative justice has spread throughout the world, with imaginative openings being developed as opportunities arise and leadership emerges.

Restorative justice in action in Canada

In Canada it is the judges who have introduced restorative concepts into 'sentencing circles'. The judge facilitates a conference, sets out the parameters of the tariff for the offence and leads the participants in a debate about the appropriate sentence. In parts of Canada the Prison Chaplaincy is involved in establishing support groups for serious sexual offenders so that they can be properly supported when they are released back into the community. These Circles of Support and Accountability have been replicated under the leadership of Quakers in England and Wales in partnership with CJ agencies (see Chapter 10 and Appendix 1).

The concept of 'Prisoner Sunday' has been developed into a week devoted to restorative justice, to help raise the awareness of faith communities to the possibility of considering offenders and victims in new ways.

Preventive work is being developed widely within the community by mediation in schools and neighbourhoods. This may be particularly applicable to bullying, disputes between neighbours and racial harassment incidents.

In the pre-charge stage there is a possibility of developing the current diversion schemes. Developing diversion for mentally disordered offenders who have committed minor offences away from the criminal justice to the health system has proved to be effective when inter-agency processes are developed.

In the post-conviction stage the closest sentence which reflects restorative justice concepts is the community service order, which links punishment to reparation and accountability.

In the post-acquittal stage there is a need to develop ways in which communities can support victims, families and those acquitted of an offence as the participants move forward in their lives.

Following the sentence there are major problems, particularly for those who have been released from custody. Reintegrating them into their communities is a difficult and sensitive task. This may include contact with the victims of the offender at the pre-release stage, building up the confidence of victims and offenders prior to the release. Strong processes for supervising and supporting this re-entry phase are vital. Canadian probation services have developed throughcare work to meet this challenge. There is also specialist support available in matters such as support to offenders convicted of domestic violence and their victims.

There are many more victims than offenders, and all have various needs. They may not have the opportunity to meet their offender, to have questions answered, to have their say and be listened to. They may not know who to turn to, thinking that they are a burden on their families and friends. They may feel stigmatised and apart from the community. These issues must be addressed as part of any restorative justice process and as part of our concern for community justice. The expectations of victims must be considered if we have any wish to repair the harm.

Restorative justice principles have much potential in the development of community policing. The problem-solving approach which the police now apply to difficult issues gives us all an opportunity to develop more self-supporting communities, with victims and offenders becoming more involved in this approach. The vision of communities taking action to inhibit and remedy the causes and consequences of criminal, intimidatory and anti-social behaviour is achievable.

Chapter 5
Restorative and community justice working

In focusing on the needs of victims as being central to the purpose of justice there are more opportunities for victims to meet with the people who have caused them harm in an attempt to answer their questions.

Victim/offender group

This was a group I attended, following a burglary in which my leaving present from Victim Support was stolen. The group contained four burglars and three victims, of whom one was elderly and two of us had young children. My daughter was six at the time, and was quite worried about the possibility of the burglar returning. One of the burglars declared that he would never dream of burgling a house with children or old people and the other three nodded in agreement. Then one of the group leaders asked, 'But how would you know if there were children or old people in the house, until you were in there? And then it would be too late, you would have already broken in and taken away their sense of security'. The silence that followed lasted several minutes, as the burglars digested this new realisation.

(Marian Liebmann)

So that the process of restorative justice can be understood, appreciated and celebrated I give several examples of stories showing restorative justice at work. There is however no substitute to being involved as a community member, as a facilitator, an offender or as a victim to appreciate the power of the process of inquiry involving respect for the truth, respect for all those participating and a consensual approach towards resolution and ending.

A pre-court mediation

A group of young men used to hang out in an underpass in an urban area, causing inconvenience to nearby residents. This included foul language, minor theft, criminal damage and urinating. One evening, unable to stand it any longer, a resident challenged this behaviour, on behalf of his family; words were exchanged and two members of the group assaulted the resident.

When they were arrested and interviewed, both offenders were remorseful and ashamed of their actions, having failed to appreciate the problems their behaviour had been causing others. They acknowledged that the assault on the resident was uncalled for and wanted to make amends.

The resident related a saga of victimisation, including abuse to his family, thefts from their washing line and fear of his children using the underpass. He recognised that his anger had boiled over on the night of the assault. After considered thought and some anxieties the parties met at the Adult Reparation Bureau. The offenders' apologies were accepted and a full discussion took place. Following the mediation session, the offenders cleared the underpass, and shared the problems caused with their peers, who in turn appreciated the harm caused by their behaviour. The victim was very happy with the outcome and there were no further problems. The case was disposed of by way of a formal police caution.

(Mediation UK)

Court-based mediation involving neighbour disputes

A man was charged with malicious wounding. This incident occurred after his son was reprimanded by the victim for misbehaving at the latter's son's birthday party. When the offender heard about this, he went round to the victim's house, picking up a steel tube on the way. An argument ensued and the offender head-butted the victim and struck him with the steel tube. Mediation and reparation inquiries revealed two separate conflicts: the surface tensions relating to this case, and also the dispute between the wives. This dispute had a knock-on effect, creating conflict between the children of the two families.

A meeting was arranged with the wives, where problems were discussed openly. The wives agreed to go back and talk with their husbands and families. This resulted in a mediation meeting between the couples, in which the offender apologised for his actions. Both sides confirmed that the incidents would now be forgotten and assured each other that there would be no further

repercussions between the two families. At court, the offender was
bound over for twelve months in the sum of £50.

(Mediation UK)

Post-release mediation

A woman and her eight-year-old son were the victims of an
aggravated burglary, in which they were terrorised by the burglar,
who received a prison sentence. The boy's nightmares persisted
and, as the time drew near for the burglar to be released, the
woman became apprehensive that the burglar would return. She
approached her local Advice Centre, who referred her to the local
Mediation and Reparation Service.

The mediators visited the offender (just released), who was
upset to hear how worried his victim still was. A meeting was
arranged at the Advice Centre, at which the offender apologised in
full and reassured the victim he had no intention of returning to
cause harm. The victim accepted the apology and reassurance, and
found the meeting helpful. The son's nightmares stopped soon after.

(Mediation UK)

A victim who wanted to meet a burglar

The victim of an unsolved burglary requested help from Victim
Support in arranging a meeting with a burglar. She was having
difficulty sleeping, and suspected all strangers, including people
at the bus stop outside her house. She had received considerable
support from Victim Support, but still had many questions as to
why her house had been chosen. A meeting was arranged between
her (and her husband) and another burglar on probation, who had
wanted to apologise to his victims, but had been unable to do so.
The meeting took place in prison, where the burglar was serving a
three-year sentence for two burglaries. The victim was able to ask all
her questions, and felt reassured by the offender's answers, because
he responded to her questions honestly, and also seemed genuinely
concerned about what had happened to her. After the meeting, she
was able to sleep well again, and go back to her normal activities and
way of life, and this was a great relief to both her husband and her
three young children. She only wished that the meeting could have
taken place a lot earlier, to set her mind at rest. The burglar in his

turn was pleased that he had been able to help someone who had suffered from a similar crime to the one he had committed.

(Marian Liebmann)

A victim's account of a victim/burglar group

After three burglaries at my home in eighteen months, I was interested to be invited to take part in the victim/burglar sessions.

I decided to go even though I wondered whether these meetings were intended to make me 'understand' the reason for the offence.

At the first session I was apprehensive and still feeling hurt and angry but as the sessions got under way the group began to relax. I found it was an opportunity to express exactly what the crime had left me feeling like. I also listened to other victims and realised they had very similar feelings, which made me less isolated.

The offenders spoke openly and related how they went about their crimes. It all seemed so organised and calculated – almost as if it was a normal daily job – and I felt all the anger bubbling up inside me again. But this time I was able to direct all this emotion at the offenders, thereby enabling me to feel that at least I had done something about the invasion of my privacy and loss of property. To have this opportunity can only be for the good.

After attending the four meetings, I personally found it beneficial coming into contact with the other offenders and I do hope that in the future they will take into account the feelings of myself and other victims if they are tempted to commit another destructive crime.

I was very glad to have the chance to participate and I hope the scheme will continue, so giving other victims the same opportunity to express their feelings and, hopefully, to reduce to some degree the crime of house burglary.

(Mediation UK)

Possession of a firearm with intent to provoke fear

Four young men were driving a vehicle and had in their possession a replica H and K rifle, which they pointed out of the window at members of the public and fired at them, although there was nothing in the chamber.

Staff in a garage were concerned and thought the youths were about to commit an armed robbery at the neighbourhood bank, and alerted the bank's staff. The police were called but the car had gone, although details had been taken.

Three of the youths were arrested at school later. The driver, and a fifth youth, who hadn't been in the car at the time of the incident, were arrested at gunpoint by an armed police response vehicle in the street.

At the subsequent conference, all the young men gave a frank account of how the incident was a silly prank. They realised how very stupid they had been. The true measure of the dawning of the effects of their actions came when the bank manager and assistant manager told their story. At the time that they were alerted, a female customer was in the bank with a very large amount of cash in her possession. She was convinced that she had been followed and would be robbed and had told the bank. Consequently, when the staff from the garage told the bank about the youths, the staff were forced to put their emergency procedures into action, causing considerable disruption to everyone in the bank.

The sergeant who facilitated the conference described the young men as 'four-year-olds being told a story by teacher' when they heard this account, so engrossed were they. The fifth youth also was able to express his fear at being arrested at gunpoint when he had no idea what had happened earlier.

The young men all gave heartfelt apologies, and asked to apologise to the bank staff and the female bank customer. They offered also to visit the garage to offer their apologies.

After the conference, the bank staff said they thought that this process was absolutely the right way to deal with the incident. It gave them the opportunity to realise that the young men were really quite nice lads doing a stupid thing. The conference has substantially reduced the fear of further attacks.

(Restorative conference, Maidenhead and Windsor, 9 June 1997)

Ultimately the sustaining of restorative justice practices will depend upon the ideas becoming integrated into practice (faith into action) and that this practice is acceptable to communities as well as those immediately concerned. Media response and political leadership will be crucial in gaining this consensus.

Pioneering a new way of justice

Two child arsonists who destroyed premises just for a dare will do community work to make amends.

Aylesbury MP David Lidington, who sat in on a restorative justice session at the old police station in Aylesbury, where the children met the victim of their crime, described the two boys as young children.

He told them the effect the arson attack had had on him, while police and fire officers told the boys the trouble they had caused for both emergency services. The boys had to try and explain to those in the room why they had caused the fire.

Restorative justice is a system of dealing with mainly young offenders, pioneered in Aylesbury and now widespread in Thames Valley, which aims to get offenders to realise the effect of what they have done on the people involved in a session chaired by a local police officer.

Mr Lidington, now [1999–2001] a shadow Home Office minister, decided to come and see a session for himself. In spite of the seeming lightness of the punishment, Mr Lidington thinks restorative justice is not a soft option for first-time offenders. But he wants to prove that it works. And he does not believe this is the answer for hardened criminals, who should go to prison for a long time.

Monday's restorative justice session must have been a difficult experience for the boys, said the MP. They seemed to have done it without understanding the consequences of their actions. By being made to explain, the boys had seemed to realise that what they had done was wrong and how much hurt they had caused.

Mr Lidington was impressed with the fairness and lack of aggression of the conference, which had been attended by the boys' parents. The boys had also realised the distress their behaviour had caused to their families. Afterwards, said Mr Lidington, the victim himself had suggested some kind of community work for the boys. 'The victim told me he found it useful and that he wanted an acknowledgement from the children that they had done wrong and done harm, but he also wanted to find a way to get their lives back on the straight.'

The boys were also given a formal caution, which will be on their records for the next five years. If they re-offend, the justice system will not be so sympathetic. Mr Lidington said this system was far more severe than merely cautioning the boys. 'I was impressed, but clearly this project needs to be monitored to make sure it's effective. It's not a panacea. And I would have lots of questions before extending it to hardened offenders. If this project can stop children getting into the habit of crime then that is a public good.' But serious crimes needed severe sentences, he said.

The principles of restorative justice will now go nation-wide under the provisions of the Youth Justice and Criminal Evidence Act, which says local Youth Offender Teams must be set up locally to look at first-time offenders and devise programmes aimed at their individual needs.

(Margaret Smith in
the Thame Gazette, October 1999)

Working together in community partnerships

A significant development in community justice is the emergence from within communities of a partnership approach between interested groups and agencies, supported by the statutory bodies, such as the police and probation services. These movements are closer to the real needs of communities and are becoming increasingly accountable to them. The involvement of faith communities in such partnerships provides for the spiritual dimension to be expressed in action.

The development of partnerships between the agencies involved in criminal justice and local community groups has been a remarkable story of successful grassroots activity, responding to the needs of the area in which they are based. Quakers at Britain Yearly Meeting in 1999 heard from Jamie Wrench about an imaginative initiative arising from the work of the Ludlow Partnership.

The local police are members of the Partnership. Before it started they had embarked upon Operation Bumblebee, which was basically a policy of harassing known criminals who hadn't at the moment committed a crime just in case they were thinking about it. As in many cases they were thinking about it, this had an impressive effect on the crime figures, although it did little for community relations and of course it did nothing to change the mindset of the people involved. It would have been easy for the local police to continue with this policy; it certainly had a substantial measure of public support. But getting your retaliation in first does not ensure long-term peace. It was followed by something completely different, largely due to the courage of two community policemen. Their names are Peter Wilson and Charles Naylor. Three years ago they decided to live adventurously, risking criticisms from politicians, ridicule from colleagues and resentment from the law-abiding majority in the town where they worked. They are not Quakers, but they embodied the principle of answering that of God in everyone.

They brought to the Partnership a proposal. In a nutshell it went something like this:

> 'We know that during the summer we shall be run off our feet chasing after half a dozen known troublemakers aged between ten and fifteen who will be causing mayhem. Last year they committed over fifty offences, most of which we can't prove. Those we can prove will take the best part of a year to come to court.
>
> 'As we are going to be involved with them anyway, we might as well do it positively. We suggest we make a deal with them. We need to remember that these kids are looking forward to a summer in which they will be drunk, drugged up, sinking the boats on the river, fighting, swearing at the tourists and generally having a good time. Whatever we offer them has got to be a sight better than that.
>
> 'In the first place, we help them build top-quality mountain bikes (using parts donated by a local firm). Then we take them out into the countryside and basically wear them out. If they stay out of trouble, at the end of each week they get a free ticket to the local centre for a swim, a ride on the flume and some chips. If they stay out of trouble for the whole of the holiday, they keep the bike. If they commit a crime, the deal's off.'

In the end the Partnership found sixteen sponsors to fund the equipment for this project. Three lads managed the whole course, and kept their bikes. The other three lasted until the fourth week; on one night they had a little spree and committed four offences. The next day they were off the scheme; their bikes were taken away from them, and they were banished.

The effect was extraordinary. The youngsters themselves were devastated, those left on the project were impressed, and the police were delighted – just for once the administration was immediate and with a minimum of paperwork. Many of us thought that, once off the project, the three rejects would go completely off the rails, but they simply hung about trying to get back on it. Reported crime that summer fell from fifty-three to four. The following year the project was repeated, but this time there were more people involved, and the big prize – rather difficult for Quakers – was a trip to the local Army training ground and a chance to drive a tank, fire real shells and engage in other war-like activities. Crime in that age group fell to zero.

This was just one of a series of community projects within the Partnership. What was the effect of its spectacular success? First, it has contributed towards the dawn of hope in an area where there was none before. The town is little by little becoming a more competent community. Second, people with other agendas stepped in. The individuals involved were congratulated officially. Peter Wilson was moved to a more prestigious post where the problems are similar and the numbers greater. Charles Naylor received a police award. And the County Council, faced with budget cuts, decided to concentrate resources on areas with (wait for it) a high incidence of youth crime and therefore drastically cut the hours of the youth workers involved in our project. Another key worker was allowed to remain part-time only after a flood of protests at plans to remove her altogether. It's a funny old world.

What insights have I drawn from this experience? First, in the fickle world of politics, long-term commitments no longer exist. It remains for other agencies, of which Quakers are one, to provide the vision, the patience and the stamina to achieve real change.

Second, these things cannot be done independently. None of the agents within the Partnership has the resources or the contacts to achieve its goals without the support of others.

Third, the effect upon the spirit of those involved can be remarkable. Many officers have become personally committed to the Partnership once their official involvement has ceased. People's spirits respond to brave acts rather than brave words.

Fourth, in the real world some of our principles must be tempered by practicality. I and my Quaker colleagues had to grasp the nettle of supporting a plan to give disaffected youngsters an opportunity to play with weapons of war. And the reality of public funding is that much of it now comes from the National Lottery. If we are to do all that we want, we are going to have to seek funds from Trusts, public services and Lottery funding.

There are also wider issues thrown up by this story. For example there was the police assertion that they knew who the 'criminals' were. But crime does not have a universality about it. A crime is only a crime if we say it is – or rather if those who make laws say it is. Quakers have frequently found themselves at odds with those law-makers. Over the centuries they have endured imprisonment for 'crimes' from speaking the truth to withholding tax that would be spent on armaments, standing up in the face of laws that are wrong because like Luther they can do no other.

But what if the laws are right? How many of us have broken laws? Parked on a double yellow line? Broken the speed limit? Driven with perhaps more alcohol in the blood stream than is allowed? I suspect every one of us has at some time broken some law. It does not of course make us criminal . . . but what if as a result of our parking an ambulance failed to reach hospital on time and the patient died? What if our speeding or drinking resulted in someone's injury or death? Are we then criminal? And if we are then, why were we not before?

Another issue is that this project almost certainly stopped some of the young people involved appearing in court. Many years ago I studied criminology at university, where I learned that the best way to ensure someone became a recurrent criminal was to catch him before he grew out of it. Researches show that almost all so-called delinquents give up by their mid-twenties *unless they have been labelled by being brought to court and sentenced.* Being a criminal is partly a matter of luck: if you are born white and middle-class, you have a better chance of growing out of it without being arrested, and if you are arrested a better chance of being cautioned rather than sent for trial, than if have if you are born black or working-class. Justice is not even-handed, nor blind: it is a fallible art, practised by fallible humans who are influenced by their own upbringing,

experiences and prejudices. And the processes of justice begin with
the criminal act, to which the public, the police, the politicians,
the media and the courts react. The response is not necessarily
measured, not always thought through, all too often concerned with
retribution rather than reformation. It is delivered through a system
designed to be fair, with built-in checks and balances, adjusted by
statute and case law, constantly evolving, but nevertheless a system
in which the individual – victim or offender – is often a passive
spectator at a complicated game in which the rules are known only
to the players, and the players' desire to win against each other
tempts them to engage in gamesmanship; to commit professional
fouls, to twist, bend and stretch the rules to breaking point and
sometimes beyond – in order to get a result.

Many Friends are involved in radical initiatives designed to
break this mould. I am humbled by their vision, their energy, and
their heroism. But most of us will not change the grand order of
things. As the Chinese proverb has it, the miracle is not to fly in the
air, or to walk on the water, but to walk on the earth.

If we start with criminal acts, and try to repair the damage they
do to the victims and the offenders, however well we do it, we still
chase after events rather than influence them. If we were brave
enough, we could start with the other half of the equation – the
people who might commit these acts – including ourselves. We could
try to discover what spiritual emptiness drives them to do what they
do. We could look for and seek to answer that of God in every one
of them. We could try to create the conditions in which the evil in
them is weakened and the good raised up. To do so requires no great
organisation or charisma, but it may require a shift in our thinking.

And remember, the greatest mistake is to do nothing because
you can only do a little.

(Jamie Wrench, Britain Yearly Meeting 1999)

*The sustaining of developments over several years is evidence of how
much they meet the needs of communities to become self-reliant and
regenerating. The experience of the Ludlow Partnership's work on the
Sandpits estate is described one year on from Jamie Wrench's account.*

The Sandpits estate in Ludlow has experienced the dawn of hope through the transforming power of vision, imagination, courage and commitment. When communities are given the opportunities of working with the problems of disadvantage and are supported by faith groups, all things are possible.

The sad story of the vandalised Baptist Church, now situated in the middle of the estate, built in 1867 on the main road out of town for farmers and labourers, has moved on. Through the persistence of the original congregation of nine, their courage in remaining and sustaining a vision of the potential of their church, and the leadership of a few, a community centre and church have been built. This centre has led to an awakening of a spirit of confidence within the area and to many changed lives.

From the shocking incident of an unsolved rape in the town came the formation of the Ludlow Partnership involving the Council, social services, education services, the police, the Baptist church and other faith communities, including the Quakers. This forum has enabled planning to meet local needs to be carried out with sensitivity, in order that crime can be prevented. Resources have been made available through the town's focus on action within the estate.

The rebuilding of the Baptist church as part of the Rockspring Centre and the appointment of Ken Paskin as the minister and overseer of the community centre in 1994 have transformed the facilities available to the community. But without the continuing encouragement and empowerment of the active engagement and ownership of local people none of the current activities of the Centre would have taken off. Indeed, when the buildings were being planned, the members of the community and the local police were warning that the buildings would not be safe from vandalism and arson.

Six years on and there have been two windows cracked through normal wear and one piece of graffiti, which was cleared up by the perpetrator at the insistence of a local young mother. The community's needs have been closely considered in developing the centre's functions. There is a real sense of ownership by people from the estate of the many functions that the building, and the staff associated with it, provide – classes (ranging from parenting skills, through GCSE English and Maths, IT for people who would not attend normal education centres, to Tai Chi), youth activity groups, counselling, play group and post-school club activity. This all happens within a building that has a church in it.

The involvement of the police in developing the particular bike project described by Jamie Wrench at 1999 Yearly Meeting has been crucial in integrating the work with other agencies. The community police attached to the project see the work at the Rockspring Centre as vital in helping the community develop its own ideas and meet its own needs. Charles Naylor and Bev Nichol value their participation in the work of the Centre and the ease with which they are accepted within the community. They are sensitive to the dynamics within the wider community of the town, and the pressures on them from their colleagues ensure they are aware of the realities of working in other policing settings. The investment the Police Service have made in the work of community policing demonstrates the benefits gained from imagination and commitment in such schemes, but also shows that there are real results to be gained from such leaps of faith.

The predominant ethos of evidence-based work, which dominates the funding of developments within the criminal justice system, clearly has led to the continued support of the scheme that started with bikes for behavers. Workers and volunteers maintain that project. There was such enthusiasm for getting onto the scheme in 1999 that several youngsters have had to be turned away. This exclusion from activity is now a cause for concern and may lead to new considerations next year. A significant development from the first year's project has been the involvement of two of those who benefited then, helping out this year. Andrew and Sam have joined as assistants and have been significant in ensuring the motivation of those involved in the activity this time and indeed into one petty theft during this year being owned up to.

The bike project has to be placed in the context of the Partnership's commitment to the Sandpits estate and the issues of crime prevention in the town. The emphasis of much more effort is now been given to preventative work at national and local level. Such a focus has been shown to be effective in solving problems rather than dealing with their results. Under the Crime and Disorder Act of 1998 all local authorities have prepared strategies to prevent crime in their areas, all have appointed staff to address the issues arising from a local crime audit and all are working across agency boundaries to tackle the action plan arising from the audit. Ludlow is well ahead of the field and is much visited by those seeking to learn.

Outstanding issues for the Partnership are the continuing issues of unemployment in the town and the growing evidence of drug and alcohol abuse particularly among the young. The Rockspring Centre is seeking to grow to meet these needs. The hope of using the recent single regeneration budget through funding for the Housing Association provides the possibility of an extension to the work of the Centre to provide a workshop area, increased child care and a youth activity centre, with appropriate staffing.

Hope is sustained through opportunities that are realisable, realistic and attractive. Rockspring provides this for Sandpits in an imaginative and remarkable way. The leadership of individuals is important in this achievement but so is the willingness of many to risk themselves in growth and change. In the minister's office next to the Sanctuary in the building, Ken Paskin (who moves to a new project in 2000) has this Old Chinese inspiration above his desk, a guide to all who seek to address social issues:

> Go to the people.
> Live among them.
> Learn from them.
> Start with what they know.
> Build on what they have.
> But of the best of leaders
> When their task is accomplished,
> Their work is done,
> The people all remark
> We have done it ourselves.

(Tim Newell)

Chapter 6
Theology, justice and forgiveness

The way we consider people who are subject to our system of justice defines our view about the nature of being human. The basic value of human nature is reflected in the way we consider those who have transgressed our expectations and are dependent upon our decisions under the criminal justice system. The godliness within each of us is reflected in the way that we can be transformed by the process of repentance and forgiveness. From this premise we recognise the potential for transformation within each person: we do not write off groups as untreatable or as evil; instead we hold out a vision of their future as members of a community which involves them within it.

Spiritual values and crime

The close connection between religion and crime and punishment has been evident throughout history. As a symbol crime has replaced sin as our society's measure of personal righteousness. As a test of this, ask yourself the following question: which would cause you the greater anxiety – to hear that the Bishop was calling round to discuss a sin he had heard you had committed, or to hear the police would be popping in because of suspicions you had committed a crime? Explorations of the concept of sin and crime are often confused and although penal theorists would say they should be separated we can identify legitimate connections. The development of classical criminology was a reaction to the idea that criminals were possessed by the Devil. Theology was considered to be old-fashioned and to have no place in criminology. Instead reason was to rule the jails and the criminal justice process. This was clearly not possible to sustain as the fundamental nature of the processes was inevitably infused with deep-seated emotions, which often overrode reason.

However the lack of 'religion' in criminology did not prevent the Victorian triumvirate of Chaplain, Governor and Medical Officer dominating jails for over a century, and the continuing influence of the Church is maintained through the appointment of chaplains to every prison. Religion and jail are inextricably linked.

The use of time in prison represents a penance to many: the failure associated with the offence can be dealt with through a resolve not to reoffend.

Repentance and forgiveness can be central to the meaning of criminal punishment. The retributivist approach asserts that punishment is justified solely by its relationship to a past offence – the criminal should be punished, as he or she deserves. That is, an injury committed merits an 'injury' in return. Consequentialists argue that a penal system must be justified by the consequential benefits particularly in reducing crime. There is an irreconcilable conflict between the two approaches; the demands of retributive desert cannot sit happily with consequential utility.

Community relationships

An alternative approach is to combine a consideration of the offender's crime and of the potential to reduce crime, in terms of the offender's relationship with the community. Punishment can be seen as an expression of the moral response of indignation and resentment. But such expression leaves offenders as objects and therefore they have no moral standing. We could consider instead the process being one of communication between two or more subjects. Thus the legal system could be seen as a means of communication with the citizen. The purpose of communication should be to gain assent; the trial would be an attempt to engage with the citizen in an inquiry to answer the charges, to communicate the condemnation if there is a conviction.

Severe treatment as a form of punishment can be challenged as unnecessary if the trial has already expressed condemnation. However, a communicative theory of punishment which seeks an appropriate response from the offender can explain the purpose of severe punishment as a penance which the criminal is required to undergo. As a vehicle for repentance penance serves a forward-looking purpose for it expresses the will to reform and it can help offenders restore the bonds of community – with God, with their fellows – which their wrongdoing has threatened. These purposes can also be served by a penance that is imposed on an unwilling wrongdoer. This can lead to the offender gradually accepting the purpose of the penance.

The consequentialist can accept this if the offender realises that the penance can bring about a change as long as the offender has free choice within this. Repentance is central to this concept of punishment. The ideal of any criminal punishment is to bring about repentance and to provide a penitential medium through which that penitence can be reinforced and expressed to others.

Such an approach to punishment could have a significant implication for the sentencer, especially the need (or requirement) to show why imprisonment, which excludes the offender from the community, is a necessary punishment for the most serious kinds of offence, but for them only; and why punishments in the community form a more effective response to many kinds of offence. Community service could be said to be the ideal form of penance. The fine is currently an under-used punishment in our culture and yet can be seen as the most immediate and understandable penalty, particularly for those with the capacity to pay.

Repentance

Genuine repentance may be one of the most difficult acts for a person, let alone a community to perform. We think of repentance as a gift of God. It is not just that we do not like being wrong, but almost invariably the others are not completely right either. But repentance demands that we should take ourselves out of the mesh of small and big evil deeds which characterise much of our social intercourse, should refuse to explain our behaviour and accuse others, and simply take our wrongdoing upon ourselves: 'I have sinned in thought, word and deed,' as the Book of Common Prayer puts it.

A person who admits his guilt makes himself defenceless and vulnerable. He is weighed down. But he can begin to be free from alienation and the determination of his actions by others. He comes to himself and steps into the light of a truth that makes him free. Liberation through confession is a painful process, but once made he has travelled some distance towards reconciliation. The next step is forgiveness.

Forgiveness

Forgiveness is no easier than repentance. Within the victim, anger swells up against the perpetrator. The angry Psalms are more readily referred to than the words of Jesus on the cross. Our sense of justice also resists forgiving – the perpetrator 'deserves' unforgiveness; it would be unjust to forgive. If perpetrators were repentant, forgiveness would come more easily. But too often they are not. And so both victim and perpetrator are imprisoned in the automatism of mutual exclusion, unable to forgive or repent and united in a perverse relationship of mutual hate.

Instead of wanting to forgive, we seek revenge. An evil deed demands instant repayment in kind. The Old Testament 'eye for an eye' was originally an instruction limiting revenge, rather than encouraging vengeance. Revenge, however, enslaves us and the spiral of vengeance seems woven into the fabric of social realities. There is a certain irreversibility about our actions which make it difficult to escape the mutual distrust. The only way through the predicament of irreversibility is through forgiveness. It breaks the power of the remembered past and transcends the claims of affirmed justice and so makes the spiral of vengeance grind to a halt. The Christian gospel centres on the role of forgiveness within human affairs. We are enjoined to forgo revenge seventy times seven. 'Father, forgive them . . . ' is the ultimate example of the revolutionary message. To forgive those who have wronged you is the act of great inner freedom. The idea of forgiveness implies an affirmation of justice – 'Forgive us our trespasses as we forgive those who trespass against us.'

Forgiveness is not a substitute for justice, but it provides a framework in which the search for properly understood justice could be followed. How can we find the strength to forgive, however? Should we persuade ourselves that forgiveness is invariably good for mental and spiritual health, whereas vindictiveness is bad? Should we tell ourselves that, given the nature of our world, it is wiser to forgive than to fall prey to the spinning spiral of revenge? How can we satisfy our thirst for justice and calm our passion for revenge so as to practise forgiveness?

In the imprecatory Psalms, torrents of rage have been allowed to flow freely, channelled by the structure of a ritual prayer. This may be the way out of a slavery to revenge and into the freedom of forgiveness. The psalms are prayers, and it is before God that the rage is placed, not in the quiet managed form of a confession, but as an outburst from the depths of the soul. By this placing of anger before God the perpetrator has begun to be included in the community of humans. In the presence of God our rage over injustice may give way to forgiveness, which in turn will make possible the search for justice for all.

The pain of forgiveness is ultimately seen in the significance of the cross and of the prayer from it. Redemption from the passive suffering of victimisation cannot happen without the active suffering of forgiveness. It heals the wounds that the power-acts of aggression and exclusion have inflicted and breaks down the dividing walls of hostility. Yet it leaves space between people that allows them to go their separate ways in 'peace' or to seek reconciliation to restore communion.

It is likely that most of us have been faced with the decision of whether we should forgive another person who has hurt us. It may have been an easy decision in which forgiveness was proper as the basis for restoring good relationships with someone we love. Other cases may not have been so easy and there will have been some anguish in deciding about forgiveness or there may have been so much pain inflicted by the other person that we feel unable to forgive even though it may seem to be the right thing to do. Ultimately we may have been hurt in ways that compel us to reject forgiveness and hold on to resentment and bitterness as the proper moral position.

Forgiveness is an important issue in our lives with our families and friends. Translating that idea to our concern with crime and punishment may not be so readily received. We seem to have overlooked the relevance of such an important personal issue as forgiveness as a suitable subject for criminal justice and yet it is in making such connections between the formal and the personal that there can be a transformation in our experience of our institutions.

Forgiving is an intense personal experience in which feeling about the other person is central. It involves overcoming our feelings of resentment about the other, regaining our sense of worth and separating the action of the wrongdoer from their person. As well as very personal issues concerning the individual, it is possible that we could hold a collective sense of resentment arising from our membership of a group that has been mistreated, even when we have not suffered any individual harm.

In overcoming our sense of resentment what do we let go? Resentment is the response we feel when challenged in our sense of worth. The mistreatment we have experienced has exposed the possibility of a lower value in ourselves than we had previously supposed. We begin to doubt the way we consider ourselves in relation to others and particularly those who have hurt us. Our resentment of them is an attempt to restructure our worldview in a way that affirms our value despite their rejection. The ignoring of the wrongdoer as someone who no longer matters is often an attempt to rebuild the person. But forgiveness gives the lie to this approach and restores the wrongdoer as someone who does matter despite his or her wrongful behaviour.

The way we deal with resentment after such pain and the diminishing of ourselves is dependent upon our membership of a community in which readiness to consider forgiveness is essential. This is the sort of moral world we all need and want. Thus each of us could commit ourselves to cultivate the disposition to forgive – not the sentimentality of forgiving any wrong, no matter how deep or unrepented, but having the willingness to be open to the possibility of forgiveness with hope and some trust.

Community safety

Criminal justice is concerned with the maintenance of acceptable standards amongst people who have no necessary connections with each other beyond social existence. Social existence, however, does commit us to an important set of relationships beyond our family, friends and immediate associates. Each person holds a relationship with other community members that is synthesised by reciprocal respect for individual rights and responsibilities. The criminal justice system becomes involved when an offender has denied this reciprocal respect to the crime victim and the community. A key function of the justice process is to affirm to the crime victim and other members of the community that reciprocal respect for rights and responsibilities is important. Its rejection challenges a key community value that confers security upon rights holders and stability within the community.

Our considerations of those strategies show that they often fail to take into account the richness of forgiveness as a moral, emotional and social experience.

A criminal justice system that seeks to affirm the value of damaged rights by relying on deterrence, censure and rehabilitation is likely to fail to address the resentment which victims, primary (those directly affected by the crime) and secondary (those who are associated with the event) experience. If a serious response is to be made to the needs of crime victims as community members whose faith in a fundamental right has been undermined, proper account should be taken of forgiveness, and victims ought to be helped to deal positively with their resentment.

Sensitive and respectful interventions by those around a victim in disputes between friends or family members reflect the concern for the difficulties experienced by the adversaries. Such mediatory intervention is not only concerned with a solution to the problem but would seek a result that positively reflected the group's core values. This would reflect a definition of wrongdoers' responsibility for the offence, but their separation, through their experience of learning, from the action that offended the group's values.

Similarly, when transferring the concept into the communal level, there is a need to affirm the value that has been threatened by a crime whilst recognising and valuing the offender's membership of the community. Resentment by primary and secondary victims, and by the community, confuses legitimate indignation about the crime with a rejection of the offender as somebody who matters to the community. The provision of criminal justice strategies that facilitate forgiveness and reintegration may avoid this problem. There may be circumstances in which the person is an outsider by choice, in which case opportunities for joining a community could be part of the process, but there must be a realisation that the individual's wishes will be respected.

Deciding with forgiveness

Any adjudicating process that we could explore should retain the opportunity for condemning the crime but include a way for forgiveness of the offender. The process, similar to conferencing but with a different focus, will require an open forum that has the following membership, functions and process and may produce the following outcomes.

Membership – The parties involved are likely to be the primary crime victim, the offender, a representative of secondary victims, a collective representative (some sensitivity is required in assessing the contribution of such people) and a mediator who is concerned to see a positive result that reflects the indignation of the community for the wrong done, as well as the commitment of the community to all its members, including crime victims and offenders.

Functions – These involve identifying appropriate indignation at the wrong committed, enabling the offender to explain his actions and offer an appropriate apology, facilitating forgiveness by forum members (realising that this can only happen when the victim is ready), assuring both victim and offenders that they are valued members of the community and determining the appropriate level of penitential punishment, aimed at developing a greater capacity in the offender for self-awareness and empathy with other community members.

Process – This should involve an open discussion about all aspects of the crime, trying to get to the truth about the events, an opportunity for the parties to express their feelings and thoughts about it, and a chance for offender and victim to communicate their perspectives on the crime both at its commission and subsequently.

Range of Outcomes – Where it is agreed that the offender has wronged the community the parties may express their critical views and their experience of anguish. The offender then may wish to make an offer of genuine apology. The primary victim and the secondary ones may then wish to express their feelings of forgiveness. Thus the offender, separated from his wrongful action, may resume life as a reintegrated member of the community. The offender may agree with the forum to undertake some penitential punishment that demonstrates his affirmation of the values that he has rejected and that he now seeks to embrace. After the completion of the punishment a further meeting of the forum may accept the apology and then wish to express forgiveness of the offender. There may also need to be a less desirable outcome where the forum imposes a penitential punishment in the absence of a readiness to agree an appropriate period of penance. A decision on forgiveness is likely to be deferred to a subsequent forum on the completion of the punishment in the hope of receiving a meaningful apology that will lead to forgiveness by the affected parties. Offering the prospect of forgiveness is not included in many current conferencing settings, but with the need for healing it should be part of the proposed model. Forgiveness cannot be forced or arranged, but it can be an expectation that we all work towards and pray for.

Within this approach are synthesised many concepts about restorative justice, mediatory developments and concepts of penitential outcome and it provides an outline of a system for maintaining offender and victim in community. There are further issues to describe in order to deal with the inevitable criticisms of the model.

Safe custody

The detention in a safe place of those who represent the most danger to the community should be a separate matter from the place where the actions of the wrongdoer are being considered in the light of the community's views. The question of dangerousness, if separated from the questions of levels of punishment and of victims' rights, could provide a full consideration of those matters that currently can be ignored under the pressure of risk management. The question of detaining a person on the grounds of dangerousness could become a civil matter, and a model of such a possibility is being developed through the work on the management of severe personality disorder. The use of preventive detention, as in the 'reviewable sentences' for those who remain a risk after they have served the punitive part of their punishment, provides a model of risk management with the possibility of building in appropriate assessment, treatment and judicial safeguards. If we can see this detention as 'protective' of the rights of the person detained, rather than purely 'preventive' as currently proposed, then the emphasis upon every person as a member of a community who is entitled to respect can be reflected within public policy. Thus our emphasis on forgiveness as a core element of criminal justice will ensure that we pay attention to the caution with which we impose protective detention and careful attention to the nature of protective custody.

The concept of deterrence is inconsistent with the idea of forgiveness in which each person possesses intrinsic qualities that are seen in a communal concern for reciprocal respect for individual rights. The use, or sacrifice, of one person for the benefit of the greater good cannot be consistently supported within the same criminal justice structure that emphasises the value of the individual in its concern with forgiveness. However, restricting protective detention and deterrent sentencing might well leave a community vulnerable to the commission of crime. Although there is not much evidence to support the likelihood of such a risk, there are potential strengths in the model of forgiveness in criminal justice in that it promotes an interactive process with crime issues.

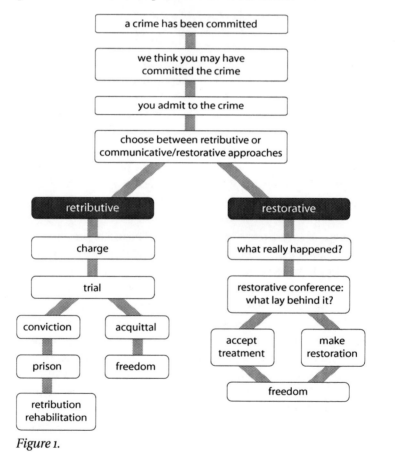

Figure 1.

The approach proposed here would require a much greater response to crime from ordinary citizens. Crime is recognised as a problem for primary and secondary victims and they have a democratic right to become actively involved in dealing positively with their feelings of resentment and the deep-based insecurity caused by the actions of the wrongdoer. Braithwaite describes this concept of community members being involved in a 'shaming' process of the wrongdoer and then of reintegrating the offender back into the community of law-abiding citizens through concerted participation. Thus citizens and communities handling their own crime problems can lead to low-crime societies. A possible choice in the manner of considering a crime is portrayed in Figure 1. Figure 2 shows the contrast between different ways of considering crime and working with those involved.

Some will resist the opportunity to express an apology, and there will be crime victims who refuse to let go of their resentment even when faced with appropriate periods of punishment and worthwhile apologies. Neither of the changes described is an easy task and an emphasis upon forgiveness in criminal justice asks a great deal from offenders and crime victims, but it also holds out many rewards. The renewed relationship can bring many benefits in freeing offenders from the effects of immoral action and releasing the victim from being trapped in the position of continually defending themselves. The model of forgiveness in criminal justice provides us with some idea about a process transformed by the values of respect and consideration of the potential in each person.

Forgiveness can be seen as distinct from punishment; as being predominantly moral whilst punishment is predominantly legal. Punishment can be self-imposed, as when offenders realise the enormity of the harm they have done. In such cases, forgiveness held out to them can be the first step in their learning to forgive themselves. The possibility of forgiveness must be central in any system that considers the criminal's repentance and the restoration of relations with the community. Forgiveness cannot ignore the serious wrong the offender has done. It should clearly lead to the offender becoming aware of the wrong, if necessary through punishment, and repenting that wrong. Forgiveness is also inconsistent with excluding offenders from our concerns, far from

Figure 2 Contrast of Three Paradigms for work with offenders

	Welfarist rehabilitation	Correctional Treatment	Restorative Practice
Causes of crime	Primarily structural, Social and economic	Primarily individual/familial	Breakdown in relationships Contextual disruption
Responsibility for crime	Primarily the State's	Primarily the offender's	Offenders and their communities of care as well as paucity of opportunities
Characterisation of criminal	Unfortunate individual for whom assistance is required	One of a deficient and/or dangerous group (classified by risk) from whom society is to be protected	People who have not been aware of their damaging behaviour and the impact of it on others
Characterisation of practice	Offender-oriented assistance and protection from further damage by the system	Public-oriented punishment, management and treatment	Community, victim and offender centred practice seeking to enable those affected to take responsibility for healing the harm
Characterisation of rehabilitation	Rights-based restoration of citizenship	Utilitarian re-education for citizenship	Putting right has has gone wrong restoring relationships
Practice focus	Diversion from cstody, practical help, advocacy, seeking opportunities	Enforcing punishment, managing risk, developing skills through (enforced) treatment	Facilitating dialogue between stakeholders to empower them to take responsibility for putting things right
Intended outcomes	Reintegration of the offender	Punishment of the offender and protection of the public	Repairing the harm for the victim, the community and the offender

the community to which they and we belong. It requires us to be willing to restore our relationships and keep an effort to maintain them. This is the difference between punishment as symbolic excommunication and punishment as penance.

Punishment's purpose

Thus punishment could aim to preserve and repair the offender's relations with the wider community. The offender has obligations but so has the community: to respond to the criminal not just as someone who should be condemned or ostracised for the crime, but as someone who must be urged and helped to repent the crime and to restore himself or herself to the community. The criminal is punished among us and by us and we must share with the system's officials the responsibility for that punishment and for trying to ensure that it is administered and received in the appropriate spirit. This places a heavy burden on the community, and it is uncertain whether we would be willing to accept it. There are signs, however, that, given the opportunity, it can happen. More of this is explored in Chapter 10 in examples of how victims are respected within open contact with criminal justice agencies and offenders.

The ideal of justice may not yet be within reach but there are concepts that we can consider as suitable for greater study – sin and penance, repentance, reconciliation, forgiveness, transformation and the kingdom of God. There are signs that when alternative ideas are given support – when people exercise discretion and seek to repair harm – then there can be a transformation of feelings of community stemming from greater trust and confidence. There is always a gap between practice and the ideal and, however difficult that ideal is to achieve, it should not inhibit the struggle to achieve it. We can then see where we fall short in current practice and then discern in which direction reform should proceed.

Chapter 7
Quaker social testimony

Quakers believe that all aspects of our lives are lived in ways which lead us closer to or further from our spiritual nature and God. This applies in our face-to-face relationships as well as to the contextual relationships defined by our social, economic and political structures. It is unusual for a theological perspective to have a balanced view of both individuals and government. Some faiths – arising at a similar time – see worldly culture (including government) as inherently evil, and attempt to retreat from the world. Others hold up the government as the ultimate arbiter of good and evil – for them the idea of civil disobedience is inimical. A Quaker position on society holds the individual and the government in mutual accountability, and both are accountable to God. Faith leads us to believe that human fulfilment comes from an attempt to live in the spirit of love and truth and peace, answering that of God in everyone. The corporate acknowledgements of the practice of those principled personal acts to which individual Friends have been led by the knowledge of the light we call Quaker testimonies.

Despite the wonderful advances in technological awareness and scientific progress there have been few developments within our social wisdom to keep pace with other advances. Family, social and community relations have been weakened by the tidal wave of market relationships. A belief in fulfilment through wealth, success and power produces damaged and damaging people, for whom we are responsible. We cannot dismiss the casualties of the market nor can we dismiss those who create the hurt and who are hurt. If we write off such people we deny the power of love to transform even violence and hatred. Our spiritual responsibility is therefore to examine the nature of society and particularly the ideas surrounding community justice, to see how far we encourage the Christian virtues of selfless love, simplicity, peacefulness, truth and a sense of the equality of all to be valued as children of God, which is the foundation of all true community.

Our testimonies of *Equality* and *Community* would lead us to challenge the inequalities in our society, the extremes of poverty which exist and which contribute to crime and disorder, through poor housing, lack of opportunity and employment. The testimony of *Simplicity* would lead us to seek to be free of dependence on possessions and to resist the influence of the market in our lives. Developing resistance to consumerism is an essential spiritual practice today. *Stewardship* implies a treasuring of the world to delight and sustain us and involves hard choices for future growth and international relations. *Integrity and Truth* have long been concerns for Friends to assert in social structures. Without truth there can be no relationship with God, without truth there is no community. Our culture needs to prize truth in every aspect of our social life. Truth in criminal justice is a valuable element particularly when considering the effect of sentencing measures in persuading the public of the necessity for them. Truth about the levels of risk people face within their locality is vital in leading towards a safer and more open community. Our *Peace* testimony stems from our conviction that God is love and there is that of love, of God, in every human. We cannot escape from a world in which violence looms large. The violence which destroys peace of mind in our communities must be a major concern; however, it is our experience over the centuries that 'to live in the life and power which takes away the occasion of all wars' is to be closer to God. The strength of the peace testimony has been something that has defined us in the eyes of others, and it is possible for us to make connections between the threat from outside our society and the danger from disruptive influences within our communities.

Each individual Quaker lives out the testimonies according to his or her own light. Although they cannot be interpreted as rules, they direct us towards a way of life that respects the individual, values community and consensus, and eschews a dependence on force to solve problems. Each testimony has a complicated history and thus although caution is necessary in interpreting them they provide a powerful inspiration against which we can consider new discernment.

Living our testimonies within the criminal justice system helps us to hold up an alternative vision of human fulfilment. We may not have all the answers and we aim not to dissent for the sake of it but to encourage a return to fundamental values despite the difficult realities of day-to-day politics. Many will share our views in which justice is an active basis for social peace and community. We hold firm to the testimony of the sacramental nature of each aspect of our lives as we sense it in God's loving purpose. So in the economic and political areas of our common life we must practise spiritual discernment, and then act.

Thus our vision of the potential within each person leads us to challenge the use of painful punishment as a means of making society safer. We shall seek to repair the harm brought about by crime rather than to exacerbate the damage by further pain and alienation of the offender. We shall seek to answer the questions, dispel the anxieties and relieve the suffering of the victim; we shall ensure that the community is aware of the future risks that remain.

The current concern of criminology can be said to be a 'criminology of the self' – making sure that we are safe, our cars and houses are protected; and a 'criminology of the other' – outgroups who are to be policed. Our testimonies challenge that vision of society and lead us to embrace 'the other' – at least in spirit if not in practice. The challenge for us is to find ways of continuing to demonstrate the value of including groups and members of society who are reviled, excluded and demonised.

The hope of Friends is that the values behind the restorative and reparative approach towards criminal justice and the treatment of those effected by crime will replace the largely retributive approach which has prevailed for too long. For this to be realised there will need to be a substantial change in opinion and practice, which are dependent upon a prevailing culture from which many current attitudes and procedures flow. We will now consider the implications of such a shift in our approach to the subject that has been said to reflect most accurately the values of any civilisation.

Chapter 8
Organisational and cultural change

I offer a model of organisational cultures that will enable us to see where to act in the criminal justice system in order to support and develop change. The model has been developed through my work with the Management School at Cranfield University. It provides us with a way of understanding complex organisations and systems facing change. The difficulty of achieving change in an organisation cannot be understood without being aware of the paradigm which holds the beliefs and assumptions grouped together into perceptual sets.

The paradigm
The paradigm is an inevitable feature of organisational life. If managed properly it will encapsulate the distinctive competencies of the organisation and system within which it operates and provide a formula for success that will allow the organisation to develop. If mismanaged, however, it will act as a conservative influence to prevent change causing strategic drift away from key objectives and will lead to poor performance.

Management of the paradigm can be achieved by attention to the organisational *cultural web* that surrounds and preserves the paradigm.

The cultural web
Study of organisations has led to an analysis of the factors that contribute towards the paradigm, or mind-set. These elements can be described as the cultural web. They are interdependent and often very deep-rooted within the life and history of the organisation. The elements are shown in Figure 3. The individual elements are explained in the following paragraphs and then related to the reality of the criminal justice system.

Power structures. *Power structures describe the functional work of the organisation reflecting the effort and drive required to carry out the work; the power hierarchy of the organisation. The explicit*

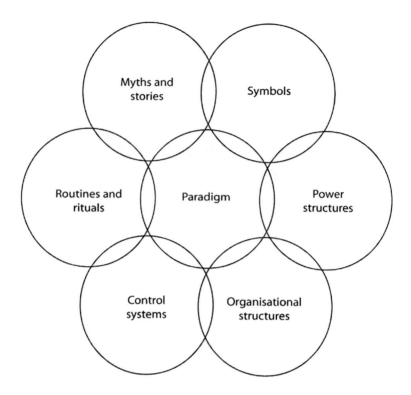

Figure 3.

structures reflect the formal arrangements as described, but within those structures are the informal power arrangements through representative and networking arrangements.

Power structures in the criminal justice system reflect the dominance of the formal institutional forces within the decision-making process. These are highly structured through the work of the various agencies such as the police, Crown Prosecution, the courts, the Probation Services and the Prison Service. This dominance represents a series of very hierarchical structures with little close communication between the elements and uncertainty about the extent to which each agency could affect the others in their decision making. Although there are signs of moves over the recent past to try to improve such communication (with the introduction of the Woolf Committees, now called Local Criminal Justice Boards, providing a forum for agencies to discuss mutual issues of concern at a local level, for example), the degree of co-operation and close working is limited to a few examples of excellence.

Since the development of the concept of 'joined-up government', or cohesive policy-making and implementation, there are greater signs that the agencies are trying to consider themselves much more in relation to each other so that there is now, for the first time, a business plan for the criminal justice system, through commitment from the Home Secretary, Lord Chancellor and Solicitor General. Through the shortening of the lines of communication and the de-layering of the hierarchies and an examination of all initiatives in line with the stated objectives of the system, the intention is to ensure that the main government departments of state will work together to provide for a safer society.

The reviews and action carried out by the government centrally have led to the Crown Prosecution Service and Prison and Probation Services working more closely together. This has been reinforced through the funding of joint initiatives through the Comprehensive Spending Review.

The emphasis on evidence-based work has demanded this focus on delivery. The power of central government has required local authorities to develop strategies and procedures to audit and address crime within their communities. Through taking an inclusive approach towards the number of agencies which have an effect on offending and offensive behaviour, it is intended that actions will develop to meet the need to improve the background factors which contribute towards the likelihood of crime in an area.

Organisational Structures. *Organisational Structures describe the formal arrangements made by the organisation to describe working arrangements. Increasingly these are flat structures with de-layered hierarchies and in effective organisations are open and organic in nature to reflect the rapidly changing emphasis of operations and priorities.*

Organisational structures remain very elaborate and complex to the extent that the decision-making in the criminal justice system is difficult to follow and accountability unclear. There are signs that such structures are being altered through the need to deliver planning and operations at a much more localised level with multi-agency co-operation. One such example is the development of the Youth Justice Board and local Youth Justice Teams, with local authorities in the lead on developing crime prevention plans through audit and the involvement of agencies such as health, education, housing as well as ones more centred on criminal justice. Another example of structural alteration is the increasing move towards agencies having the same boundaries in order to encourage closer responsiveness to each other's and public needs. Although there remains a strong centralised policy-making dimension, there are signs of increasing developments within regional structures taking place.

Control systems. *Control Systems monitor the distribution of resources and often constitute hard plans for the future work, defining priorities and key indicators of performance. They also contain soft systems such as induction programmes for staff joining the organisation and the appraisal system that connects individual commitment to the work of the organisation.*

Control systems in the criminal justice system are closely determined from the centre, and increasingly so with the developments in the Probation Service, where between 2002 and 2006 a national service (NOMS) has replaced a county-based organisation with considerable local accountability and involvement. This service has policy and standards developed from the centre but is retaining local partnerships for the delivery of services within structures which became coterminous with police and Crown Prosecution boundaries. Thus, although there are signs of centralisation, the development of local links with other criminal justice agencies may well lead to closer co-operation and working links between agencies in order to meet the needs of local communities.

Control systems have been developed through targets being set by the government from the centre to provide performance indicators at a time of rapid change in priorities and direction from recent legislation. The three-year funding of certain initiatives under the Comprehensive Spending Review has provided a strong control system that could lead to the move towards preventive strategy through developing 'offending behaviour' programmes in the community and in prison institutions. The emphasis on reforming youth justice will create a culture change should the emphasis on diversion and earlier intervention to support and supervise individuals within their social and family settings have the impact intended. The emphasis on evidence-based effectiveness in the criteria for achieving funding for many of the projects places a considerable control upon their development and delivery as the continuing resourcing of work is dependent on showing that the aim has been achieved in terms of changing behaviour to reduce offending. The development of accreditation standards stemming from the 'What Works' evidence further introduces controls upon agencies in that funding is often dependent upon achieving such demanding standards to achieve the goals relating to effective programmes. The development of information technology systems that connect all the criminal justice agencies is being planned. This will create a control of data that is unprecedented and may lead to greater focus on the outcomes required by government policy. The introduction of the three-year planning and financial cycle provides a more flexible tool for planners and should enable longer-term implementation decisions to be considered.

Control systems can be seen at work in the way that victims are treated within the court system, which is process-oriented and focused on the offender and institutional interests rather than repairing the victim's harm. There have been moves to make the process take account of the impact of the offence upon the victim, but there is still a long way to go before the victim's needs can be seen to be respected. The victim's concern quite often is to do with why certain events happened. The justice system's focus upon proving whether something happened, and who did it rather than why, leaves the victim frustrated and unheard.

Routines and rituals. *Routines and rituals are often not described formally but are of day-to-day significance and reflect important* *relationships and activities. They reflect what an organisation celebrates and rewards in small but significant ways.*

Routines and rituals are strongly seen within each agency, as the process of administering law and order has become subject to endless rules and protocols, in order for the number of decisions which go towards the delivery of justice to be subject to the latest learning from precedent, and to reflect the requirements of natural justice. The dominance of the dynamic of reducing risk informs many routines. Undoubtedly the Prison Service has been dominated by the need to improve the record of security lapses which occurred in the mid 1990s and caused the tightening-up of procedures and systems to the exclusion of all other considerations.

The legal system is surrounded by rituals from the historical beginnings of law and retains some of the traditions that set it apart from those who use its services. Attempts to change the rituals, such as the abandonment of the judicial dress, have been met with much opposition, and others, such as the equality of access to courts for solicitors to plead, also caused much concern from one of the most established of the professions. It is perhaps in the Police Service that there is most responsiveness to change because of the close interface of their work with public needs.

Classic examples of routines and rituals are those typified by the institution's daily routines which serve the needs of staff rather than prisoners: the rituals of bag searching, the herding of visitors, the defining of areas where prisoners have no access and the time table of daily activities often determined by the meal break times which staff take.

Myths and stories. *These are the stories told amongst members of the organisation about themselves and the whole. They describe the kernel of truth about the organisation; reflecting the values that prevail and which are perceived as dominant.*

Myths and Stories are often centred on the worst aspects of the criminal justice system. Some of these are matters we take for granted, such as the inevitability of sending a serious offender to prison on the assumption that punishment is necessary. 'Something must be done about the problem of crime.' 'Prison works.' Then there are the stories that prison is too brutal and leads to more suicides because of the deprivations experienced, as well as the stories that prison is too comfortable and is no deterrent and thus many keep returning. The stories of the changed lives, despite the deprivation, struggle to be heard.

There is a great need for this area of criminal and community justice to be addressed with more exposure to an open reporting about conditions and a closer examination of the research about the effectiveness of the system which would reveal serious deficiencies in decisions we take for granted. It is in this area of myths that the vital importance of the criminal justice system provides a system of communicating certain values to the community and a background of knowing where the boundaries of acceptable behaviour are. In Britain the myth of judicial infallibility has been exposed by significant miscarriages of justice in the cases of the Birmingham Six and the Guildford Four. The fact that eventually injustice was exposed leaves a possibility of improvement for the future. There is a need for a myth of safety within the community for the stability of relationships and a sense of belonging.

Symbols. *These are the significant elements that the members of the organisation recognise as standing for them. They can include the leaders of the organisation and often include symbolic acts of particular significance and include physical features – logos, uniforms, standardised design and architecture.*

Symbols about justice are everywhere one looks at the system. The arrangement and layout of the courtroom, the level of paper-work which dominates process, the language of bureaucracy and the dress which those working in agencies prefer, all may reflect, express, denote, highlight and embody the values of the organisation. They have often popularly been concentrated upon the harsher aspects of the system, such as the prison gate with its inevitable shutting on the mind; the uniforms and corporate symbols of each agency are designed to give confidence and some sense of stability. The uniform of the prisoner sets him or her apart from us. The image of the stocks remains a symbol of shaming and public exposure which many look back on with a sense of regret that that sort of experience is not available now. The ultimate symbol of the gallows remains a strong macabre image in the public conscience. More modern symbols being developed include the electronic tag, the increase of community groups coming into prisons to use facilities and the development of the role of prisoners taking responsibility for helping other prisoners in schemes such as the Listeners (for the potentially suicidal).

Achieving change

Traditionally strategic change within an organisation has focused on the first three elements – power structures, organisational structures, control systems – as being the most recognised and easily influenced areas of work. However, it is often the case that the latter three elements – routines and rituals, myths and stories, symbols – may resist strategic change, particularly if it challenges their existence. In order to be effective strategic change must affect all six elements of the cultural web. Managers and those who seek to reform should address all elements over time in order to ensure that the change they perceive as required has a lasting effect and is fully incorporated into the life of the organisation and leads to a change of the culture.

The cultural web can be used to identify what features of the criminal justice system must be addressed if change is to be brought about successfully.

There are clearly some areas where it is possible to detect changes in the elements of the cultural web that may contribute towards the change in the *paradigm*. The original paradigm was centred on the need to protect the public (or an elite and powerful section of the public) through a careful consideration of the risks offenders represented. The means through which this risk was considered reflected the culture of retribution. The change towards a more restorative paradigm or culture can be seen to be emerging in some aspects of our approach towards community justice. The process through which this is done will afford the individual more power to accept responsibility and to influence the outcome of the process in a more direct way than ever before. There are signs that a major paradigm shift is possible as we realise the potential of greater movement in the culture within which offenders and victims are considered.

In the next chapter a further consideration of one of the major elements of the cultural web – myths and stories – will be explored as we work towards possible areas for action. Each element of the cultural web has the potential for such consideration.

Chapter 9
Working with cultural change

In Chapter 8 I made a case for a many-faceted approach to bringing changes to our criminal justice processes. Working with one of the concepts, that of myths and stories (which describe the kernel of truth about an organisation), may give us a way to develop the work.

Previous work on restorative justice has stressed the differences between that and conventional retributive justice so much that we feel forced to choose between the two – as in Figure 1 on page 84. After describing some of the cultural myths at the heart of our society's current response to crime we will consider the possibility that slight shifts in these myths can open up possibilities for mergers between restorative and conventional criminal justice.

As Friends we like to focus on the positive aspects of human life. But if we want to exert influence on the practice of criminal justice we need to present a credible analysis of the problem of crime. Our prescription must take into account that human evil is also pervasive. At the social level, this requires us to recognise the ways that social conditions – poverty, violence, and inequalities of power and opportunity – destabilise social harmony and breed criminal behaviour. We need to begin to see criminal activity as one of a number of expressions of unresolved conflicts within society. Punishing one criminal does nothing to stem the generation of crime if the social malaise that nurtures crime continues unchecked. At an individual level, we need to be prepared to hold people responsible for their actions while at the same time we should acknowledge that not everyone's capacity for personal responsibility is developed to the same degree.

Myth one – the scapegoat
The origins of the myth of the scapegoat in Old Testament culture are seen in the ritual by which the sins of the community were rested on the sacrificial goat. What happens to the status of the scapegoat when the role is held by a human being? In order to function as a scapegoat the person needs to be defined as the embodiment of

wickedness. Any acknowledgement of goodness would interfere with his or her function as the bearer of the community's ills.

René Girard has described the essential role of the scapegoat in resolving conflicts. The feuding herdsmen could unite in venting their anger on the scapegoat, thus ensuring harmony in the community. We see scapegoating exercised today, for example, when a nation that is split by internal wrangling comes together in time of war to unite against the common, external enemy. Part of the 'criminology of the other' is the assumption that the offender (or 'criminal') is the common, internal enemy. As such, the criminal is required to assume the same identity or role as the scapegoat.

In recently filling out a reference for the partner of my son I was asked to certify that she is of good character. The main criterion used for the certification of 'good character' was the absence of a crime on one's record. The public clamour against the released sex offender, or the difficulties any offender has in finding employment once their record is known, testify to the strength of the scapegoat myth in modern society. Within criminal justice itself, the myth finds expression in many practices. One example is the tendency in policing to go first to a known offender when a crime is reported. Within prisons, the twin priorities of security and control exemplify the view that a prisoner is never to be trusted.

Scapegoats and redemption

If the myth of the scapegoat is to be challenged from within criminal justice, we need to show a more balanced assessment of the offender's character. We need, first, to counter the view that people who do not have a crime on their record are totally innocent while anyone who has ever been arrested is totally wicked. Solzhenitsyn in 'One Word of Truth', his Nobel address, wrote, 'If only there were evil people somewhere insidiously committing evil deeds, and it were necessary only to separate them from the rest of us and destroy them. But the line dividing good and evil cuts through the heart of every human being. And who is willing to destroy a piece of his own heart?'

The understanding that there might be something good in an offender is emerging, gradually, in all the ways that empower offenders. In prisons, for example, the service of a prisoner as a Listener would have been unthinkable not so long ago. Prison policy was resistant to any work by which one prisoner would have a privileged position over another. What stood in the way of the prisoner Listener was the belief that anyone convicted of crime would take the opportunity offered by hearing of someone's pain to exploit the prisoner thinking of self-harm. Instead, Listeners are proving that empathy is a basic skill of effective work with desperate people in prison, and a fellow prisoner is likely to have more empathy with the pain of another. There is certainly much closer sympathy between prisoners about the distress they experience within the custodial setting and a greater likelihood of credibility in relating to each other given the opportunity to develop appropriate caring roles. The shared experience of deprivation makes for strong bonds of common emotion. Particularly in settings of long-term prisons, the development of a sense of community can be effective in providing for the care of the individual prisoner as well as the well-being of the group. There are similar dynamics at work in the increasing involvement of prisoners as key skills tutors in educational tutoring. The same holds true in drug treatment work, where many of the most effective counsellors are former drug users and prisoners.

Myth two – banishment

The power of the scapegoat myth came from the fact that the goat, bearing the sins of the whole community, was sent away, exiled. The prison functions as a means of banishment for modern society. One of the roles of the prison in the banishment myth is incapacitation – the possibility that prisons make society safer by enabling us to remove those who would do us harm. Although practitioners in the system are well aware of the turnover of prisoners, the wider society holds on to the myth that sending someone to prison solves the problem. At its extreme, people would appear to believe that no one ever comes back.

One of the expressions of this belief is the opinion that prisons ought to be made much tougher to deter others from committing crimes. This employs the myth of perpetual banishment in two ways: first, it does not seem to matter how bad the conditions in the prison are – if we assume that the people inside will never get out. Secondly, the emphasis is on deterring others, as though (scapegoat myth again) those inside are incapable of rehabilitation.

Most people would be shocked to find out how quickly the average prisoner is released after serving a sentence. Part of the reason for the quick turnover is the limited number of cells. In order to imprison today's armed robber, yesterday's robber must be released. Hence the image of prison as a human warehouse is inaccurate. A far more telling picture is the revolving door. If the impact of prison on offenders is beneficial, then society is helped each time the revolving door turns. If, however, the prisoner comes out embittered after experiencing victimisation and humiliation, then each turn of the revolving door is to society's detriment.

The myth of banishment – that sending the evil away from us forever can solve society's problems – can thus lead to two opposite views of prisons. One is that prisons need to be made as horrible as possible to become better deterrents. The other is that banishment through prisons damages people and we would be better off without them anyway.

The redemption of the myth of banishment needs to begin from a third possibility. Prisons are not inherently damaging, nor is incapacitation a realistic means of reducing crime. In the middle is the possibility – manifested in much current mediation practice – that prisons can serve as a 'time-out' in situations of serious conflict between the person and the wider society. One of the ways that prison already serves this function is that people who have serious drug problems can make use of their time in custody to de-toxify. But prisons could also function as places of 'time-out' in other ways – for example, where families have been torn apart by domestic violence. What is needed for prisons to achieve this function is a move towards treating the prisoner as a responsible citizen, to play a key role in his or her transformation and reintroduction into society.

Myth three – punishing the guilty solves the problem
Much of the investment in criminal justice practices and systems is dedicated to finding out who is guilty and administering their punishment. The deep attraction that punishment poses for many people is the belief that it brings to an end the pain and instability caused by crime. The feeling that the sentence brings the situation to a fitting conclusion shares with the scapegoat myth the idea that all the blame rests on the person who was found to have committed

the crime. The sense of finality may be linked to the idea that prison is for ever.

The myth is composed of two central elements: first, guilt rests on an individual who has acted wickedly; and secondly, imposing punishment on the guilty is the end of the problem. The first element is deeply embedded in western society. An individual sense of guilt is tied up with our liberal economic systems, according to which each citizen prospers or fails according to their own efforts. It is true that one can be found guilty of conspiracy, in which case we entertain a sense of shared guilt. But conspiracy is not typical of the cases before our courts and, more important, it simply broadens the model of individual guilt to encompass criminal gangs who are treated as one individual.

To challenge the myth of individual guilt we need to broaden our sense of shared guilt or responsibility, so that accountability becomes a matter of mutual duties in a community, bound together as the 'kingdom of God'. The concepts of citizenship and fellowship may help in developing this sense and experience of community.

Shared responsibility points to the moral duties society owes to the most disadvantaged amongst them. Herbert Morris has written of communities too callous to provide decent housing, education and support for families, or medical care. He is not saying that we have to let off criminals because what they did wasn't their fault. His point is that we in comfortable society have made a material contribution to fostering the conditions in which crime increases. This means that we, society, failed the young offender when we expelled him from school. It means that, when he comes back to the magistrates on another charge, his failure to honour the terms of his probation order (for example) is balanced against the possibility that society failed to support him in his efforts to stay away from crime. For example, has he benefited from the kinds of opportunities for work or counselling that might be given to a middle-class schoolboy who has experimented with cannabis? Finally, are the laws to which he is held accountable fair? Have we been fair to the cannabis-smoker by criminalising his behaviour when his father can drink to excess with impunity?

One of the reasons police officers and prisons are needed to serve society is that we as a society have not addressed some difficult issues. There are many people in prison who would not have been in custody but for society's unwillingness to invest in support, treatment, care, counselling, mediation and refuge.

The second element of the myth that punishment brings the problem to an end follows a satisfying emotional cycle. The mythological sequence seems to start with fears upon the discovery of a crime and then the pain that it caused; followed by the central mystery: who done it? This is followed by the tension leading up to the arrest, the titanic struggle between good and evil played out in the courtroom and, finally, a sense of conclusion and relief when the sentence is passed on the guilty one.

The finality myth is attractive to a broad range of people. Victims often express a hope that no one will ever have to suffer the kind of pain they have been through. Retributionists bring a sense of a 'job well done' to meting out punishment to one who has been proved guilty. The police, who have to respond to the damage caused by a troublesome offender, can breathe a sigh of relief when he is (temporarily) incapacitated.

The kernel of truth in the finality myth should be that when someone has served their time, paid back their debt to society, the offence is cancelled and he or she will be welcomed back. However, it is precisely this aspect of the myth that society fails to deliver. Instead of prison as the end of the matter, society has begun to see cycles of crime and has become more concerned about repeat offending. A few years ago, the view that sending someone to prison brought the problem to an end was replaced by a concern for the offender's resettlement, culminating in open prisons specifically designed to enhance prospects for employment and re-accommodation. At the same time, the harm that punishment itself imposes was taken into consideration, with more attention to the needs of prisoners' families. In these ways, the evidence that the punishment causes problems of its own was taken seriously. Victims, too, expressed dissatisfaction with the outcomes of the criminal justice processes. The police, the courts and the prisons were not reducing the incidence of crime, nor were punishments compensating the victim for the pain suffered.

Advocates of restorative justice have been quick to point to the aftermath of a crime as evidence that the system is backward-looking. However, the expansion of effective programmes which address offending behaviour and treatment for drug and alcohol dependence in prisons shows that the criminal justice system can adapt to a growing concern about what happens after punishment. Here again is evidence that the criminal justice system can merge its objectives with those gained from restorative justice. The 'finality myth' should not be rejected – but it needs to be re-shaped.

Where crime is seen as a conflict – or as a symptom of conflicts – within society, we should be seeking ways to resolve the conflict. Crime does inflict harm, and the problem is never solved while the pains felt by the victim persist. But the opportunities for making amends through restorative justice practices can bring genuine resolution. And just as the criminal has an obligation to make amends, so society has obligations to support him or her in ways that encourage that reintegration. The 'finality myth' suggests that when a crime is committed the goal of society should be to find and punish the guilty one. Current criminal justice practice, informed by restorative justice principles, shows that the goal of society ought to be reparation of the harm done and rehabilitation and reintegration of the person who committed the crime.

Chapter 10
Ideas in action

Enabling direct communication between individuals and groups that in the past were represented through the criminal justice process has become the most exciting development in recent years. This contact gives victims the opportunity to set the agenda and seek answers to the questions that have worried them since the trauma of the crime. The following account asks some fundamental questions about the purpose of justice.

Elizabeth had been a cashier in a supermarket when five masked men entered the store and robbed it. One of the robbers forced a knife to her throat, screamed and threatened her.

Elizabeth was so frightened that she lost control of her bowels for a long time. She couldn't sleep, believing that the robber would know that she had spoken to the police. Her colleagues thought her predicament humorous, unable to understand why she should be so affected. Her bulimia returned. Matters got worse and Elizabeth was barely able to get four hours' sleep each night, regularly suffering from nightmares.

The police caught the team of robbers, but the 'criminal justice system' failed to keep Elizabeth informed about the progress of the case. She received counselling and it became clear to her that she really needed to learn from the robber himself what his intentions were towards her and her family. The robbers were represented by counsel, and pleaded guilty. None was called upon to give evidence or to give an explanation for their behaviour: their counsel acted for them, and their punishment was reduced for the plea of guilty.

Elizabeth's fear did not diminish. She set out, therefore, to try and see the robber in prison. After two years an interview was arranged and she learnt first hand that the robber always made such threats when committing a robbery and that he had no intention of harming her. The robber, for his part, for the first time, came face to face with the fear he had generated and heard just how he had wrecked Elizabeth's life.

They both benefited from the experience. Elizabeth now sleeps normally and has recovered the full control of her body. In her words she is 'healed'. The robber has changed too; staff at the prison feel it was a maturing experience and estimate that he is less likely to reoffend.

The issues raised in Elizabeth's experience are pertinent to those who have been victims of crime. The feelings of frustration and dissatisfaction are common and can be shared with those in the family and within the community. The traditional justice system focuses upon blame and pain in considering:

- What law has been broken?
- Who has broken it?
- How should the offender be punished?

Restorative justice considers:

- Who has been harmed?
- What is the nature of the harm?
- Who is responsible for that harm?
- What can be done to repair the harm?
- How can the person responsible put things right for the harmed person now and avoid harming others in the future?

(Robert Davies, Assistant Chief Constable,
Thames Valley Police)

On February 2nd 1990 Ruth Moreland was murdered by Andrew Steel (not his real name) in her home. Ruth's mother Lesley attended the trial in January 1991 at which Andrew Steel was sentenced to life imprisonment. Lesley wished to meet Andrew, and it took till December 1995 for the meeting to be arranged. Extracts from Lesley Moreland's manuscript, now published as An Ordinary Murder, *describes some of, describe some of the dynamics involved in the meeting.*

I had plenty of time to think about why I wanted to meet Andrew Steel.

Firstly, I wanted to find out more about what kind of person Andrew Steel was and what had been going on in his life before he killed Ruth. I had never heard his name before he was charged with her murder. Because he had exercised the right not to give evidence at the trial there had been no opportunity to form any first-hand opinions about him. The police had told us that he had a history of violence towards women and that he had broken a previous girlfriend's arm. They had tried to get some of the women to give evidence but they were too frightened. The police had painted a picture of a young man whose behaviour was anti-social; in addition to the violence he was a thief and drug abuser. At the trial, the defence evidence included information about problems at school, he was bullied, he suffered from asthma. But apart from hearing his response to the charge of murder and acknowledging his identity we hadn't even heard him speak.

Secondly, I wanted to hear from him directly, in his own words, what happened and why he thought he had killed Ruth. I realised that any explanation would be likely to be incomplete and might raise as many questions as it answered. I could see that there were risks in that he might tough it out or say hurtful things about Ruth. His action had a major impact on my life, on all members of my family and many other people. I felt he owed me an explanation. I recognised that any meeting could not take place against his will and indeed it wouldn't have any value if he were coerced into agreeing to it.

I wanted to ask if his family were in touch with him and if they were supportive and how they were coping.

I wanted to know if he was getting any help and if he had any plans for when he left prison. Was he being given any training or educational support? My greatest fear was that he might be released and kill or harm someone else once he was released if he didn't know the impact of his act or left prison without the necessary skills to establish a new, non-violent life.

And finally, I wanted him to know that despite our great and ongoing grief about Ruth's death, our lives were continuing constructively. This was my agenda for the meeting with the Probation Officers. While I couldn't 'act' a part, I wanted to present myself as being calm and reasonable. What I didn't want to share at this meeting was my hope that if I met Andrew Steel I might be able to say that I could forgive him for killing Ruth.

The meeting with Andrew Steel took place in Gartree Prison in a

private room with a probation officer and a friend of Lesley's present.
Andrew was struggling again but he looked as if he wanted to say
more.

My mum says that she will never forgive me for what I done to
Ruth. She finds it hard to come and see me sometimes.

What was he looking for? Sympathy from me? I said that I had
often thought about his family and hoped that in time his mother
would come to see that what he had done was one part of him but he
was still her son.

Can I say something? My expression is not showing tears
outside. It is inside. I cry every night. Ruth did mean a lot to me, she
was a very close friend. I will never forgive myself. I still read the
letters your mother, Joy sent me. Sometimes I sit there and look at
Ruth's photo, from the articles in the paper and I try to take myself
into what happened. I try every way I can so one day I can actually
talk about it. The pain I have caused you and your family I regret. I
do feel ashamed of myself for what I have done. I am. Sorry.

He could 'never forgive himself' and his mother had said she
will 'never forgive him'. Could I forgive him? No, I couldn't and I
didn't say anything except to acknowledge that I could see that he
was sorry. But what was the sorrow about; it seemed to be more
centred on feeling sorry for himself. He cried every night. 'You and
me both, sunshine,' I thought.

He must have sensed that I was finding it hard to accept his
apology as he said, 'I hope that one day you do believe me'. It wasn't
that I didn't believe him, I did believe that he was sorry that he
had killed Ruth and he was sorry for the impact on her family and
friends. What was his concept of forgiveness? I didn't feel we had a
common understanding and it would take time to establish and time
was running out. I sat, stony faced, struggling to find something not
too harsh to say and yet with honesty so I said, 'I do appreciate this
meeting and that you are saying as much as you can.'

*Later in the meeting Andrew Steel was asked how he was
feeling.*

'Scared, ashamed, there is no ending. I'm glad you came. What
pushed me more was to understand your feelings, what happened to
you and your family. I've got to be able to understand that and never
let anyone else go through that.'

The time was up. I wanted to let Andrew Steel know that I recognised and respected his courage in going through with the meeting and that I did feel that he had done his best to give an account of what had happened. I couldn't say I forgave him. Could I bring myself to shake his hand? If I offered he would extend his dominant hand, the hand that had taken Ruth's life.

All four of us stood up. I said, 'Thank you for coming.' And offered my hand. He took it and we shook hands before he turned and left the room.

Back on the train to London I felt drained and exhausted, not sure yet what the overall effect of the meeting had been. I did feel relieved. Relieved that at long last the meeting had taken place. Relieved that it had achieved the objective of meeting Andrew Steel and now being able to see him as a person rather than as a cardboard cut-out character identified only as a murderer. Relieved that he had been able to talk and that he had given an account of what had happened which tallied with the information I had already had. He hadn't resorted to lying; I felt that he had done his best to give me the information I needed. He had said he was sorry and I hadn't made that an expectation so that was a bonus. I was also relieved that the meeting had used all the time allowed and that I had not wasted time by getting upset or angry. And yet, I hadn't been able to forgive him.

There was a sense of achievement that despite the many obstacles I had got through the 'system' and achieved what I wanted. It had happened in a way which meant that if anyone else wanted to arrange a similar meeting in that prison it should be easier for them and for the prison staff and offenders.

(Lesley Moreland, 1999; 2001)

Since Lesley Moreland's meeting in Gartree prison the protocol for visits between victims and offenders has been developed. Guidelines include the preparation procedures for both parties, the need to establish clear time scales and maintain them, and the expectation that there will be only one meeting arranged so that the time is focused. The pioneering work of brave victims has begun to make it safer for all to proceed to arrange such meetings. A further example of a meeting arranged through the perseverance of a strong person follow in Lorraine's story.

Keith Stanley – the man who had murdered my father and destroyed my family.

He had been in my thoughts almost every single day for the past ten years. If I could ask him just one question, what would it be? How could I choose one question, when I had so many? I had to meet him; it was just something I had to do.

The only way to do it was to get him to agree to me visiting him. So I wrote thinking I would not even get an acknowledgement.

Three days later I had a reply; not only a letter, but also a visiting order. I could not believe that after all these years the door into the unknown was open. This was going to be either the best or the worst thing I would subject myself to. But I had to do it.

For the next few days I thought about my decision. The hardest part was having nobody to share this with, as I could not possibly tell my family what I was about to do. I was still in two minds whether to go or not. Keith Stanley had stated in his letter that he too had thought about my forthcoming visit throughout the day after he had received my request. He said that my interests must take priority – whatever my reasoning. He also said that he thought it must have taken a lot of courage and humanity for me to make contact under the circumstances, when a rebuff might easily have extended my hurt.

He too wanted me to keep thinking about it before I actually faced him. I expect he was just as apprehensive as I was.

I did not tell him why I was doing this, or what I wanted to know. I did not know myself at the time, but I guess deep down inside I wanted to know what happened that night, and why he and Harry Wood had shot my father in the face with a sawn-off shotgun, while he was sitting in his lounge.

After sitting through the trial for two weeks, there were so many missing links. I just had to have the chance to ask some questions myself.

A second letter arrived. I began to get worried as my request must have come to the attention of the authorities because of who I was and what my reasons might be for writing to Keith.

At first they would not allow me to visit in the normal way. They asked for the visit to be held in a private room with a probation and prison officer present. Keith did not agree to this. He thought it would not be the best atmosphere for us to talk. Therefore, the prison eventually allowed the visit to be held as normal.

My mind was made up and the day had come. There I was stood outside HMP Kingston (Portsmouth). He had only been an hour away from me and I had no idea. I had originally written to Long Lartin Prison in Worcestershire.

I stood outside looking at the enormous wooden door. It reminded me of television programmes, yet this was real and I had to go inside.

The time in the waiting room seemed like an eternity. I was so scared reading all the signs and procedures on the posters on the walls. Everyone in that room seemed to look at me as if they knew it was my first time.

Finally we were called to go in and I went through the security check and the door was locked behind me. I was very aware that all the staff knew exactly who I was and looked at me sympathetically. I was so frightened, and I felt like I was a criminal. What was I about to experience?

I was the last into the visits room and everyone else had sat down. I could not see him for looking. I started to panic inside. I was fighting the tears, scanning the room. Then, all of a sudden, there he was standing looking at me. He had not changed at all. The man I remembered from when I was a child, who had the cheek to be smiling at me! I could not look him in the eyes and my hurt had now changed to anger and resentment.

After the initial introduction, I asked the one question that haunted me 'Do you regret killing my dad?' He replied, 'The second your dad died, my life ended.'

I did not know what to believe. I tried to read more into his answer by looking at his facial expression, but it was all too much at that point. I asked him if he could tell me everything that happened that night. He agreed, and started at the beginning. He was so candid that shock took over from grief.

I had always thought that he had fired the first bullet and so he had been the one to end Dad's life. Yet as I listened, the story began to unravel. Wood had apparently shot him first and by Keith Stanley's account this seemed quite plausible. My whole attitude started to change now. My feelings and outlook on this incident started to change – it seemed to make things easier to find out that Wood had done it. I had never liked that irrelevant little man anyway, but Stanley I had known since November 1979. He had been an employee of my father for years, and in my eyes then he was a nice, kind man to me. I guess that is why I found it so hard to accept that he could have cold-heartedly taken my Dad away from me.

I asked many more questions that helped me piece together that night, but I can never understand why it all went so far, and why they killed him knowing that he was all alone in the house with my four-year old brother. How could they have done that knowing that my brother would wake up and discover?

Visits were closing, and we were only half way through the story. I had to know everything and was faced with having to ask if he would accept another visit. He agreed and told me to go home and apply for another visiting order.

Three weeks later I was back. The fear was not as great this time, yet when he started to talk again he no longer showed so much remorse or shame. This time I no longer felt in control of the conversation. He was now blasé and made me feel as if I was there for his benefit and not mine.

We had come to the end of the events of the night my dad was murdered and there was still an hour left of visiting, so I asked some trivial questions about him and now the answers were not what I wanted to hear.

He still had a marriage and a home to go back to – his family visits him on a regular basis. His children still have their father and his three grandchildren are able to see and grow to love their grandfather. He can repair and rebuild his life on release. I can only try to continue to come to terms with what was so violently taken away from me overnight and can never be replaced. My whole life was changed that night by someone who had no right to take another's life.

Throughout this deep discussion with him, I also discovered that my family kept so much from me, possibly to protect me, but their action has done nothing to help me or ease the pain. Honesty is by far the best policy, regardless of the pain and hurt. That way you learn to deal with what has happened and to come to terms with such tragedy. I will never accept it, but hearing the other side enables me to form my own opinion.

After putting myself through all of this, I do not regret it for one moment. Facing one of the men who killed my father was the hardest thing I have done. By doing this I now feel that I can lay some ghosts to rest and start to progress with my life that has been in remission for ten years.

Maybe this is not everyone's answer in these circumstances, but after years of being unable to deal with such trauma, it has helped me.

(The names in Lorraine Nolan's story have been changed.)

In Canada an inspiring piece of work is being developed, using the principles of restorative justice in a very practical and sensitive manner. The involvement of faith communities has been critical in such work.

The idea of the Circle of Support and Accountability for released sex offenders came from a cry for help from such a man released at the end of his sentence with no formal support links in place. The project developed in Ontario through the Mennonite Central Committee under contract with Correctional Services of Canada. They have developed a manual to help to train and support the volunteers who make up the circles.

The Community Reintegration Project (CRP) forms a 'Circle of Support and Accountability' with a potentially high-profile sex offender re-entering the community after serving a full sentence in the prison system. More and more such offenders are having no statutory supervision when released. (This is not the case in England and Wales, where all currently sentenced long-term prisoners get some post-release supervision.) The concern is to minimise the risk to the community, particularly children. The needs for victim's healing are also recognised, as are their feelings of vulnerability and their fear that the ex-offender will violate someone close to them. The Circle holds the ex-offender accountable to the terms of his voluntary commitment to responsible behaviour and a predetermined course of treatment. The Circle protects his rights as a citizen, and helps him cope with the reaction of the community, police and media. Intensive support is offered round the clock.

In the past with the release of high-profile sex offenders there had been considerable community turmoil, but to date (2007) in Canada there are over 60 ex-offenders being reintegrated into communities through the use of a Circle, with three or four reconvictions.

The community bears some of the responsibility for the safe re-integration of ex-offenders, and the Circle enables this to happen. Circles are mainly drawn so far from faith communities. The commitment could be a long-term one and may continue for several years.

The Circle strives to provide a safe and healthy environment for the ex- offender by fulfilling many roles.

- Circles function as advocates, serving to increase the level of co-operation with police, neighbourhood groups, victims and treatment providers.
- Circles serve a critical purpose in confronting the ex-offender about attitudes and behaviours that are anti-social or pro-criminal, and which put him at risk for relapse.
- Circle members are there to help walk the ex-offender through emergencies.
- Circles, as a concerned subsection of the community as a whole, are involved in mediating community concerns.
- Circles are there to help the ex-offender celebrate anniversaries and achievements in re-integration.

(CRP Newsletter Autumn 1999)

Arising from the Canadian experience, Quakers have led a project in the Thames Valley and Hampshire since 2001 to develop Circles of Support and Accountability. There has so far been only one reoffending – for breaking and entering – out of more than 30. An account of one man's circle shows the process at work.

John is a man in his fifties and has served four years in prison for indecent assault against his own two daughters. John had heard about the Circle Project from his Quaker Prison Minister and having arrived alone and isolated into the Thames Valley area upon release referred himself to the Project. Although John had committed acts of incest and was assessed as a level 2 category of risk, his psychometric profile relating to deviancy was significantly high. This high deviancy profile fitted with the history of the abuse in that it began when his children were babies and continued until the eldest was twenty-one. John had undertaken extensive sex offender treatment while in prison and was involved in a community-based treatment programme. He had appeared to take full responsibility for his offending and had good awareness relating to victim damage. John's Circle consisted of

- a youth worker (male aged 40, married with children)
- a housing officer (female aged 20+, single)
- a therapist (male aged 75, single)
- a student social worker (female aged 30+, single with children)

While in prison, John had discovered he had a talent for art and during his sentence had won an award for his artwork. The first time the volunteers met John he brought with him his portfolio. Feedback from volunteers had been that this had helped allay their fears over this initial meeting (most of them had never met a sex offender before). It allowed them to immediately see John as a person with talent and qualities. Meeting regularly, John shared the work he had undertaken in prison and was currently undertaking in the community-based programme. The Circle identified issues relating to John's under-assertive nature and discussions followed relating to the pertinent issue of passive aggression that had been a feature of his offending behaviour. John enrolled in a number of courses at a local college and found he had a skill for creative writing. The Circle began individual contact with John and it was clear that a basis of trust and friendship was being established.

After a year of the Circles' work project staff conducted a review. During this review one of the volunteers stated that a long-term relationship had recently ended and in recent weeks John had been a source of great support to her. Project staff, initially alarmed at the possible implications of such a statement, found upon further exploration that appropriate boundaries were being adhered to and that what was taking place was a genuine positive relationship.

The fact that she had confided in John and allowed him to support her emotionally in an appropriate manner had validated the relationship as real and gave him a feeling of self worth.

The relationship John had with all his Circle volunteers was a close one and was particularly meaningful to the 75 year-old therapist. This volunteer openly admits that his motivation for becoming a Circles volunteer was a mixture of factors. Abused himself as a child he was interested in the subject matter both professionally and personally. He perceived himself as a humanist and believes in the principles of inclusion and restorative justice. He also stated he was lonely.

After two years of the Circles life John completed his course in creative writing and secured a place at University to undertake a degree in the same subject. Following this news Project staff received an email from one of the volunteers questioning whether the move from college to University would affect John's contextual risk. Such a question within the context of such a strong Circle highlights and validates the effectiveness of what a Circle can achieve. The result was arrangements made for the Circle to meet again on a formal basis to help support (if needed) John make the transition.

The downside to this Circle is that two years on John relies heavily on his Circle for friendship. The issue of the Circle acting as a facilitator to helping develop outside networks of support has been discussed but has so far produced little result.

(Hampshire & Thames Valley Circles of
Support & Accountability 2005)

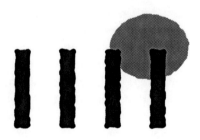

Chapter 11
Proposals for a way forward

Applying faith through understanding

There are certain principles which will assist in developing a way forward and which are recognised in current good practice:

- Criminal justice should have a well-defined and limited role to play in any democratic society.
- Civil justice is based on the principle of restitution and therefore is more in keeping with our theme.
- Depenalisation should be the aim for all societies.
- Private, for-profit prisons are likely to lead to pressure to increase the use of imprisonment and therefore should be opposed. They are a way of buying off collective responsibility and accountability that are those of the state exercised on our behalf.
- Respect for human rights should be asserted to include all members of the community.
- Criminal justice systems should work to include women and ethnic minorities working at all levels of their operations.

There is within the slogan 'Tough on Crime, Tough on the Causes of Crime' an opportunity for us to explore the possibilities for the future and how we can contribute to the shaping of attitudes and practice. What is proposed is that we should use our vision of the kingdom of God combined with the experience of developing communities as safe places in which to live. The view we work with must reflect the complexity of the subject. There are no easy solutions to the deep-seated issues concerning the causes of crime. That is why we should welcome a commitment to tackling them, recognising that it is not the individual we should be tough on; rather we should address the social systems around the person, which affect group behaviour and limit opportunity for the person. Thus the emphasis on crime audits, local strategies and youth justice groups recognises the multi-faceted aspect of social breakdown and criminal behaviour in such a way that there are solutions at hand. Without an open approach to addressing structural issues to do with the common services within the environment which support growth and change in an inclusive way, the efforts to focus on restorative relationships will be hampered.

Within such an atmosphere of hope for future social possibilities and a political commitment to seek an integrated approach to the development of safer communities, there is an opportunity for the relationships between affected parties to be reconsidered. The experience of forgiveness within personal relationships has an important significance for all parties. We have probably all been called upon to forgive and most of us will have asked others to be forgiving. Forgiveness is an important issue in our lives with our families and friends, but would we accept that it could have such relevance in our concern for community justice? Some further examination of its potential within criminal justice systems may well be helpful in connecting the spiritual with the practical within the context of developing ideas about the nature of our society.

The criminal justice system as we experience it now, and particularly its dependence on the penal solution to the problem of what we should do with the most difficult of those who come within its remit, is based on strong theological concepts. These could well be ready for transformation. The symbolic ritualism of the system that we have considered earlier is dependent on the concepts of the process of sin, guilt, punishment, expiation, reparation, forgiveness and reconciliation. It is this series of processes which help us to understand the dependence we have upon the penal solution and how, by considering other forgotten and neglected concepts of reparation, forgiveness and reconciliation, we might have the possibility of a significant paradigm change.

There are many alternatives to custody available: indeed it is only if we cannot reach reconciliation that we should resort to our ultimate solution. We have lost the capacity to work with the full cycle and have ended much of our work at the stage of punishment. Thus offenders find it often impossible to feel that their past damaging acts have truly been written off, or that they have made reparation to their victims and their community. They often feel unforgiven and so can find it hard to forgive themselves, and thus the possibility of reconciliation with their community can be even more difficult for those who transgress. The emphasis on exclusion within our procedures continues all the way and defines our approach in relation to other cultures and systems.

Let us consider a culture shift. If we take the majority of issues of bad irresponsible behaviour that are dealt with by the courts, out of the criminal justice system, we could begin to develop the inclusive community we seek. Thus in criminal justice matters an international new agenda is emerging to challenge governments and people to consider the changes necessary to reduce the dependence on prisons and to begin the paradigm shift from punishment to prevention. Major cultural shifts in organisations and systems have come about through a combination of an acceptance that the idea is right, but also because it makes pragmatic sense. Thus the abolition of slavery was campaigned for by many who considered it a moral issue, but it was perhaps when it also became an economic issue in the southern states of America that the anti-slavery movement achieved its targets.

The consideration of the shift from punishment to prevention is timely because many people are now ready to implement tried and tested procedures to divert people from the criminal justice system. There is also an awareness of the economic and social consequences of including in the sentencing repertoire an extended use of custody because this is costly both financially and in terms of families and social groups. When we consider the process of culture change which will inform our search for areas in which to act, there is some evidence from the way in which the approach to crime is being considered through an international agenda that could confirm our approach.

There is a clear understanding about the world wide nature of the penal crisis. There are now more than eight million men, women and children in prisons throughout the world. These prisons are isolated from society and easily forgotten. There is little monitoring or independent inspection. Human rights abuses, including overcrowding, unhygienic conditions, lack of food and medical care, the spread of infectious diseases and deaths in custody, violence and corruption, are widespread. The lack of trained personnel, inadequate resources and poor co-ordination in the prison and justice systems in many countries lead to long delays in dealing with complaints and rendering justice.

There are disproportionate numbers of racial, ethnic and other minorities in prison and an over representation of the poor in most prison systems. The total number of prisoners has been dramatically inflated by the use of imprisonment in an attempt to deal with the problem of the use of drugs in society. In some societies more than 50 per cent of all prisoners are detained for non-violent drug-related offences. Ironically, similar percentages of prisoners are thought to continue to use illegal drugs while in prison. Vulnerable groups, such as women, children, juveniles, mentally and terminally ill prisoners, the disabled, the aged, ethnic and religious minorities, foreign nationals and political detainees, often do not receive the special attention they need. Many of the existing successful alternatives to custody are not generally understood by the public or used sufficiently by the courts and criminal justice professionals. Imprisonment is often used even for petty offences as a punishment of first instance rather than of last resort. The death penalty is still used in a number of countries, and those on death row often spend a long period of time in inhumane conditions without access to the rights of due process of the law.

The magnitude of these issues prompts serious consideration of how change and improvement can be brought about. There is an understanding that penal reform is an essential part of good governance; also that penal reform cannot proceed without changes to the criminal justice system as a whole which must be refocused upon crime prevention if it is to succeed. In dealing with poverty and the disadvantaged it is vital that justice should be accessible and that there should be penal reform. The recognition is growing that drug abuse is usually better dealt with inside the health or social welfare care system rather than the criminal justice system, especially when there is no violence involved.

A new agenda is developing internationally to address some of these issues. The International Centre for Prison Studies is pioneering this work, which researches international prison practice and provides a sound base for the development of best practice in prison regimes and organisation within criminal justice systems. The agenda is based on the assumption that criminal justice should have a well-defined and limited role to play in any democratic society. It should not be used to resolve problems that are not relevant to it. Depenalisation should be encouraged wherever possible with an insistence that imprisonment should be used by the courts as an exception rather than a first option. This should apply especially in respect of pre-trial detention and judicial custody. There is a growing recognition that private, for-profit prisons are likely to result in pressure for an increased use of imprisonment and therefore should be opposed. Respect for the human rights of everyone in the criminal justice system should be afforded, particularly of the victim and the accused, and a non-elitist system assured that treats all people equally. The development of healthy criminal justice systems should include women and ethnic and minority groups at all levels of their operation.

In considering how the agenda could be developed there are likely to be strategies which allow matters currently dealt with in a criminal justice setting to be resolved under other formal or informal procedures. Greater numbers of offenders who are at present in custody are likely to be dealt with in the community, and this should lead to a reduction in the prison populations. This should enable prison staff the opportunity to assist prisoners to use their time in prison positively and to prepare for release.

The new agenda which is being developed by those seeking to work towards the change in the paradigm contains consideration of the following issues:

- restorative justice
- alternative dispute resolution
- informal justice
- alternatives to custody
- finding alternative ways of dealing with young people
- dealing with violent crime
- reducing the prison population
- the proper management of remaining prisons
- the involvement of civil society in penal reform.

I will now expand on these key themes in order to consider their applicability in our experience and setting.

The new agenda in action

Restorative justice challenges the formal criminal justice systems
that have marginalised victims of crime and have failed to oblige
offenders to face up to the damage and harm that their actions have
caused. The basic principle of restorative justice is a determination
to restore the balance between the victim, the offender and the
community.

Restorative justice should be adopted in appropriate instances
as a preferred form of criminal justice process because it strengthens
the social fabric and is likely to lead to a reduction in levels of
imprisonment and reconvictions. In order for this to happen, the
public must be made more aware of its benefits. Similarly training
in the principles of restorative justice should be carried out in law
schools and for those already in the criminal justice systems. The
good practice developed in different systems should be widely
disseminated.

Alternative dispute resolution provides options that may take
disputes out of the penal justice arena and help the parties to resolve
them with the assistance of a neutral person, such as a mediator.

The mechanism for alternative dispute resolution should be
participatory and voluntary, and should take account of human
rights and gender issues. With public awareness programmes the
participation of communities, potential users, local representatives
and governments could be achieved. More training in the skills
necessary for alternative dispute resolution will be necessary to
make the system more available to potential users with gradual
recognition as a valuable and legitimate component of the rule of
law.

Informal justice contributes to improving access to justice in a
manner that is reconciliatory, inexpensive, intelligible, participatory,
and sensitive to language and value of local communities. Its
emphasis on restorative and compensatory outcomes is a useful
complement to the previous two strategies.

Informal, customary and other community-based justice which
accords with human rights protections laid down in international
instruments such as the UN Convention on the Rights of the Child,
should receive recognition and support from governments and
where appropriate should be incorporated into the formal systems.

This would enable the whole system to be more user-friendly and accessible to the poor. The danger has to be recognised that community-based justice might make use of means that do not meet the requirements of legal systems and human rights. We must take care that such justice does not become violent, self-serving or irresponsible.

Alternatives to custody can be considered in addition to the strategies outlined above, in order to deal with the inappropriate use of imprisonment which has led to widespread prison overcrowding.

Legislators, the executive, the judiciary and the public need to understand what alternatives to custody involve so that pre-trial detention and short-term sentences can be replaced by non-custodial alternatives. The rights of victims should always be taken into account when alternatives to custody are being considered. More training should be offered to everyone involved in the process of imposing or implementing alternatives to custody. Civil debtors should not be imprisoned but should be dealt with through non-custodial options.

Alternative ways of dealing with young people as required by the international instruments, such as the UN Convention on the Rights of the Child, stress that they should be imprisoned only as a last resort. This means that there has to be an alternative strategy for dealing with young offenders.

A co-ordinated and comprehensive response to young people's offending should be pursued with a wide range of schemes for the prevention of youth crime. The developments within restorative justice are particularly appropriate for young offenders. A comprehensive assessment of the young person at the point of arrest may well lead to more diversionary opportunities. When custody is inevitable, the basis of the whole regime should be rehabilitative.

Dealing with Violent Crime is so crucial for society that special strategies need to be developed to deal with it. Violent crime requires both short-term and long-term solutions, with the latter having priority. This should include preventive measures designed to change public attitudes, to encourage political dialogue and to remove economic and gender disparities. Recognising that in the short term certain numbers of violent offenders need to be imprisoned, we should look for a variety of alternative methods for dealing with them while in custody which are humane and in accordance with international human rights. As most violent offenders will eventually be released, they should be encouraged to face up to the crimes they have committed and to acquire skills which will help their re-integration into society. When violent offenders are released and it is necessary for public safety that some record should be kept of their whereabouts, this information should not be used in such a way as to prohibit their social integration. The sex offenders register currently operating in England and Wales is an example of how paedophiles in particular are monitored once they have been released.

Reducing the prison population is called for by international instruments on the treatment of offenders seeking the minimum use of imprisonment. In addition to the above strategies that will contribute to this end, further steps should be taken to reduce the inappropriate use of imprisonment.

A planned reduction of the population is preferable to ad hoc amnesties. The reduction can be sustained only by a programme of public education to increase awareness of the limitations of imprisonment as a way of protecting society. We must devise methods of evaluating the effectiveness of the police and the courts which do not rely on numbers of persons arrested and incarcerated. There should be a strict limit on the length of pre-trial detention. Non-custodial penalties should be genuine and effective alternatives to imprisonment. The use of effective pre-release methods should be promoted and drug abusers should be diverted from the criminal justice system into the health care system.

The proper management of remaining prisons which should always be run according to the relevant international standards, as established by the United Nations. In addition, there are a number of features that should be common to all prison systems.

The prison system should be regarded as a public service and should be transparent and open to public scrutiny. Standards should be set for prisons covering all areas of activity, including matching numbers of prisoners to places available. All prisoners should be given the opportunity to work, and this should not be demeaning or punitive. Prisoners should be properly prepared for release.

The role of civil society in penal reform is crucial in any long-term change. No strategy for penal reform can succeed without the involvement of civil society. Governments should recognise the need to involve civil groups in all stages of criminal justice process. These groups, such as non-governmental organisations, academic institutions and religious groups, should co-operate with each other in the interests of penal reform. There is a need to educate public opinion, and contacts with the media should be developed so that they have access to all parts of the criminal justice process including prisons. Local community organisations should be encouraged to scrutinise prison conditions and to contribute to prison activities. There should be encouragement for the human rights of those in custody and of victims to be monitored and reported upon. Non-statutory groups should be involved at local, national and international levels to promote penal reform, in such matters as legal aid, legal education and training, community services, litigation, lobbying legislators, community policing and information about best practices.

From punishment to prevention as a paradigm

As well as developing a wide agenda across several key issues at national and international level, it is possible to consider the paradigm shift from a punitive approach to a preventative one by seeing the system in primary, secondary and tertiary systems.

The *primary* systems involve work directly with the behaviour of damaged offenders in which the values of inclusiveness are worked through. These systems involve such work as mediation, community service orders, probation supervision, treatment programmes for those with severe personality disorder through therapeutic interventions either on an individual level (as with the work of Bob Johnson now being developed and promoted by the James Nayler Foundation) or at institutional level with the sort of therapeutic community environment provided by Grendon Prison. The provision of 'What Works ' programmes is a positive assertion that change is possible if people are taken seriously and respected by the development of work of the highest standard.

Secondary systems include the changes in systems of organisations such as the prisons, probation, police, the Crown Prosecution Service and the courts. The way that these agencies work together for the benefit of victims and offenders in restoring communities fractured by crime will determine the support for long-term change in our assumptions about how we should consider the most damaging people in our midst. The statutory agencies are beginning to work more acceptingly with the more focused voluntary organisations that also work for the benefit of victims and offenders. Thus groups such as NACRO, Victim Support and the Prison Reform Trust work in critical areas of need and although not part of the system are subject to it.

Tertiary systems are the social structural aspects of our life that we know all contribute towards the environment within which the focus can be taken from the individuals concerned. We can give more attention to the setting within which we can develop our communities of care and respect.

Research has shown that there are links between adverse early life experiences, such as physical and sexual abuse, with personality disorder and other forms of difficult behaviour. Poor parenting, poor living conditions and poor educational experiences are all contributory factors as well, although not directly causal. We need to address these long-term issues through long-term initiatives that will need much support to succeed and be seen to contribute towards a more stable community. There are initiatives taking place on family issues, parenting, early years education, care systems, schools exclusion policies; on drugs, youth offending and on mental health services – all these developments should help reduce personality disorder and serious anti-social behaviour in the medium and long term. The signs are that these matters are being addressed and that we could support and develop many of them within our own localities. I describe some of these in Appendix 2.

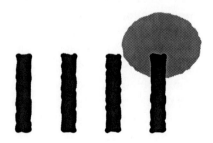

Chapter 12
Towards a Quaker vision of community justice

Working in a context

A possible model, which I have described, needs to be linked to current practice and potential in order for us to see a way ahead. There are many other groups working hard at reforming the system. Quakers should listen to their agenda. Thus the Penal Affairs Consortium, to which Quakers belong, provides a forum for many organisations to meet. The Restorative Justice Consortium similarly involves agencies and organisations with which Friends have worked closely to stimulate consideration of this fast-developing area of practical action.

We can learn much from the experience of communities that have developed procedures of acceptance and forgiveness. Therapeutic communities have as a mainstay of their work the need to be permissive in order for behaviour to be experienced and expressed so that learning can come from it. The Truth and Reconciliation hearings in South Africa clearly have much to show us about how the most painful and damaging of behaviour can be explored, understood and accepted. In this way communities can continue to live together. Canadian experience of faith communities working closely with criminal justice agencies, to seek the re-integration within the community of released potentially dangerous sex offenders, has been our inspiration and challenge and using these ideals there is scope for more leadings to work with those affected by crime in a direct way (see pages 115 and 137).

A community of citizens

Reparation goes beyond mere material compensation, for it involves the repairing of damaged relationships between citizens. The relationship between citizens has an important moral significance involving responsibilities, commitments, values, expectations and accountabilities. Without this relationship people would not be living as members of a shared community, but as individuals who may or may not benefit from the prevailing criminal justice system. Reparation in turn leads to the possibility of reconciliation that brings offenders back into the fold as fellow citizens of the community. Punishment has been seen to be a secular form of penance. The pain required is not justifiable in terms of its effect on other potential offenders, or in terms of satisfying the community's quest for vengeance, but ultimately in terms of its success in bringing offenders into a sequence of repentance, self-reform, reparation, and, finally, reconciliation with their fellow citizens.

Communicative punishment within restorative justice requires there to be certain responsibilities of citizens in whose name punishment is carried out. These include the use of law, which can be said to be as much the law of those deemed offenders as of those who sit in judgement, and the existence of a real moral standing which law-abiding citizens can claim in calling the law-breaking ones to account. The ideas represented here can be worked into the current thinking about criminal and community justice developments. The political vision includes a concern with the welfare of all members of society, and sees welfare as the realisation not only of preferences but of socially acknowledged interests and values which transcend the preferences of individuals. The concept of the person is one that recognises human identity as a fundamentally social construction and recognises the extent to which we discover and develop our personhood, personality, preferences and needs in a social setting.

The principal functions of punishment within this political vision would be to underpin the norms of the criminal law, to ensure that the community's values are taken seriously by sending out clear messages about those defining social values. The symbolic dimensions of punishment would therefore be central to its justification. This emphasis on symbolic expression over instrumental effects of punishment has implications for how penalties are imposed. As the effect of penalties would be meant to be symbolic, there are arguments for mitigating the present severity of the scale of punishments.

This communitarian approach towards criminal justice would focus on the social responsibility for crime. Thus the adjudication of breaches of a more minimal criminal law would be seen as providing an opportunity for reflecting social responsibility for the law and its impact on the community and citizens as well as on the offender's responsibility. The questions about whether criminalisation can be justified, whether the conflict or infraction can be tolerated without real danger to the community would continue to be asked. Public institutions such as the courts would find a broader set of questions about crime and society being considered.

Although these ideas may be in conflict with much of current practice in our society, there are signs that they have been at work in certain parts of our justice system. The area of juvenile justice for much of the twentieth century saw the demand for retributive punishment tempered by a concern for the broader social implications of youth crime. It has been clearly recognised that there is a need to ensure that the penal process does not reinforce young people's likelihood of breaking the law by taking a stigmatising approach. This approach provides the basis of what could be seen as an 'interpretative' way of considering penal theory. This approach starts from the practical experience of trying to keep young people as full members of society when considering the infractions for which they appear in front of the authorities. The developments within the Crime and Disorder Act (1998) have given greater scope for the wider interpretation of this approach, which should be carefully considered and celebrated. Through the experience of acknowledging the wrongs of victims, and in creating a genuine possibility of reintegration, which we have seen at work in examples of restorative justice, it is possible to use the critical tools provided by the communitarian approach. Thus there are working examples of the ideals we seek.

Community and prisons

Relating communitarian ideas to the practice of imprisonment will give us some implications of working through the principles into practice.

There is clear evidence that much of our practice would be found wanting in a system seeking to maintain and respect fundamental community values. Thus any inhumanity in prisons would be seen as counter-productive, both symbolically and instrumentally. Such a system would cover prisons with overcrowded conditions; those where there is little respect for prisoners in maintaining relationships outside the prison and for occupying their time usefully inside prison; complaints and disciplinary procedures of uncertain efficacy and fairness.

Communitarian ideas would consider the facts of crime and disorder within the prison, in terms not only of riots, assaults on prisoners and staff but also of the violence inherent in the reality of coercive custody, the inevitable impact on relations within the institution. This search would break down the attitude that crime and violence within or implicit in the prison is society's concern and calls for solutions which are pro-social in approach and impact.

The emphasis on 'prisoners' rights' in reforming prisons is questionable from a communitarian perspective. It has been argued that prisoners should retain all rights that are not explicitly removed through the reality of custody. But as soon as people are incarcerated they are in a very powerless position in which the idea of rights is very limited. More fundamental questions should be addressed about the nature of the prison regime and its effects on human autonomy.

We should also be considering the damaging effects of imprisonment as shown by empirical research and our own experience. If the impact of imprisonment on offenders is to make it more likely that they will offend again, then it is clearly a counter-productive institution. Thus for many offenders prison would be ruled out as a sanction when communitarian principles are applied to the issue.

The relationship the prison has with the community must also be a cause for examination. Geographical location and architectural structures emphasise the exclusion of the community and the inward-looking nature of the institution. Prisoners' families, friends and other visitors often have difficulty gaining access to the prison. This isolation allows the prison to operate as a kind of internal exile, which in turn allows the community to ignore our responsibility for the existence of the prison system. This can be reinforced by the geographical and social isolation of prison staff. As imprisonment raises issues of social as well as individual responsibility, all of us have to accept social and political responsibility for prisons, and to open them up to community scrutiny and accountability.

Prison changes

Some consideration about how prison life could be democratised would follow from communitarian principles. Participation and empowerment would be key themes of prisoner development, through education programmes, training and employment within the prison. Prisoners' status as citizens would thus be respected.

The accountability of those running prisons to the wider community should be considered by opening up prisons to more inspection, with the possibility of local government involvement and setting up interested community support and contact groups. A prison's accountability would be increased but it would also be much more part of the community.

Those who are closely involved with prisoners would be given close consideration under communitarian principles. The punishment which imprisonment brings to innocent parties would become much more closely examined and taken into account.

We should reappraise the role of those who work in prisons, examine the work of prison officers in particular and carefully scrutinise the work of controlling other human beings through systems of repression. The training of staff would be carried out to provide integration of systems of security, education, welfare, therapy, working and other activities in the prison. The current perceived hierarchy between different tasks in the prison would thus be reduced, removing a possible source of conflict in the work of prisons, enabling a wider social evaluation of the Prison Service's work to be carried out.

Punishment's purpose

The model we could work towards is one in which punishment is imposed to maintain the social values of the community. In the first instance this would mean using a symbolic form such as statements of judgements and warnings in courts, with apologies and means to recompense where direct victims are involved. These forms of punishment can have meaning only in a setting of shared understanding of values and an acceptance of minimal shared identity. In cases of serious and persistent crime, community service would be the major type of non-symbolic punishment. Imprisonment would be imposed in serious cases where the behaviour violates the community's most fundamental values. Such instances would be serious violence against the person and violations of sexual integrity. The impact of imprisonment on offenders and their associates would not be disproportionate to the harms caused or threatened by the offence.

Such a debate about punishment can proceed, however, only on the basis of a shared commitment to the reintegration of offenders in the community. The fact that this goal has been abandoned in the divisive laws of Britain and the United States should not deter us from looking for signs of hope in a bleak environment. Nor should it stop us from holding up the possibility of another approach which has been shown to work, particularly so in developing countries.

Realistic approaches

The focus is upon developing a humane and peaceful environment and conditions of solidarity and mutual support between citizens, which provide the public culture necessary for the development and expression of human autonomy and welfare. The advantages of the civil libertarian approach will need to be carefully developed in preserving the claims of individuals (understood in terms of their social relationships). In moving from the ideal to the actual we will need to understand the role of crime and punishment in our social order. This understanding will be enhanced by our experience of working at the issues within our communities to address what really effects our lives.

The many restorative justice initiatives in our criminal justice system at present provide Friends with a unique opportunity to apply the mediation and conflict management skills which are a reflection of our testimonies in action. The work of Alternatives to Violence Project within prisons and in communities provide a vehicle for such learning, as do non-violence training programmes such as Turning the Tide, developed by Quaker Peace & Social Witness. We could apply our energies towards a specific piece of work in order to demonstrate our beliefs in action, as we are doing in several areas already. Through the development of crime preventative strategies in each local area we can be involved in contributing to community justice. There are many ways in which we are already doing this through Community Justice Groups and other work. We should celebrate our successes and build on them.

As 1999 Britain Yearly Meeting's minute 22 stressed, it is through 'deeds rather than words' that we can make a real difference to the vulnerable and excluded, and to have a real impact on the values and attitudes which politicians and professionals bring to bear on criminal justice matters. Friends can accomplish some of this in their capacities as professionals and volunteers in secular organisations. Established Quaker projects such as Glebe House, and the Parliamentary Dialogue Group give us further opportunities to make a difference in direct ways but also by providing a model for others. The expectation of more initiatives from many Friends has led to the publication of the Crime and Community Justice Information Pack at Yearly Meeting 1999. The recommendation that there should be local Community Justice Groups to assess local possibilities and callings would, if implemented, give focus to the contribution Friends could make in their locality. The development of annual 'community safety plans' which councils in England and Wales are now statutorily required to draw up provides all of us with a chance to advise on action which will make a difference. These plans could significantly change the way crime is dealt with in Britain, and although the statutory agencies will be taking many leads in forming them, there is a unique opportunity for us to reflect on the real needs of our communities and work towards their improvement.

Practice

'Spiritual growth often comes about as a result of engaging in social action' confirms minute 22. Our experience of faith in action is that it is in the practical engagement, rather than in the thinking, planning, wishing and imagining, that we experience the growing. Through the legacy of discerning and courageous Friends, and others who have risked themselves, we have a profusion of small practical actions that can give us 'the dawn of hope', described at Britain Yearly Meeting in 1999. Through our own offerings we will really learn what it means to do 'community justice' and to understand how inseparable it is from other aspects of our social testimony.

The alternative conception of punishment that I have proposed is one informed by communitarian rather than liberal ideas. I have asserted that punishment is a process of communication between the community and offenders. The development of this concept would enable us to see how punishment can be appropriately imposed by citizens on their fellow citizens in certain circumstances. Communicative punishment within a restorative process is specified by the four aims of repentance, self-reform, reparation and reconciliation. Given these aims, communications in the form of merely formal declarations would not be effective. Repentance involves the remorseful acceptance of guilt, and this cannot be induced simply by someone pointing out that one is guilty if one has not felt any remorse up to that point. Equally, self-reform is not a process that a wrongdoer is likely to undergo without experiencing some kind of external pressure or influence.

What we could work towards is a clearer definition of our ideal. Our belief in the power of love through the process of forgiveness in communities, and a conviction that our experience of non-violent community, attainable through truth, trust and consent, provides a model and network all over the country to develop local initiatives of engagement with emerging opportunities within current justice systems. In this way we can become more human by being of service to others.

Appendix 1
Circles of Support and Accountability

Circles of Support and Accountability have their roots in restorative justice approaches to meeting the needs of those who have offended, those who have been victims of crime and their communities of care. They provide an alternative and yet complementary approach to traditional justice processes. (See also page 58 'Restorative justice in action in Canada'.)

Restorative justice is based on three main principles that can be applied to the work within Circles:

1. The principle of **repair** – justice requires that we work to heal victims, offenders and communities that have been injured through crime (the work with offenders and helping them to build their communities has been motivated by the need to avoid any further victims. Many of the volunteers who make up the Circles are survivors of abuse.)

2. The principle of **stakeholder participation** – victims, offenders and communities should have the opportunity for active involvement in the justice process as fully as possible. (Communities as represented by volunteers were not thought to have much place with sex offenders in the past, but this work has shown that to be effective in integrating ex-offenders, that dimension is critical.)

3. The principle of **transformation in community and government roles and relationships** – the relative roles and responsibilities can be rethought, and this might be the most challenging aspect of restorative justice. In promoting justice, government is responsible for preserving a just order, and community for establishing a just peace. (This principle is well demonstrated in Circles work where the community has taken much responsibility in exercising accountability and has been trusted by the agencies to work in this way.)

The work in England started in the year of moral panic following the riots in Portsmouth which arose from anxiety about a paedophile living on an estate. Learning from the imaginative work carried out in Canada led by the Mennonites, Quakers saw that this fear and hatred of sex offending and offenders can best be worked with by recognising the anxiety and demonstrating that by providing opportunities for growth and learning, the offender can sustain the change to active citizenship and the community can accept the person back with a greater awareness of the risks involved. It is good to be able to report on the effectiveness of the dedicated work that has gone into this project and to welcome the way it has been recognised widely as effective practice. It now has the potential to become a standard part of integrating sex offenders into communities over the next decade.

Circles of Support and Accountability, a scheme for helping released sex offenders not to reoffend by using small groups of trained volunteers, has now been piloted in the UK. Quakers have been involved since 1999 in promoting the concept and in 2001 the project was funded with the Home Office, covering the Thames Valley area. The project there is a partnership of Quakers with Thames Valley Police, Probation and Prisons Services. A total of 30 Circles have been established, each with one 'core member' (offender) and about four or five volunteers, a significant number of whom are Quakers. With increased funding for 2005/6, two additional Circles Coordinators were employed. The office base moved to Didcot. Helen Drewery, based in Friends House in central London, line manages the team.

There were initially three Home Office-funded pilot programmes, one managed by Quakers in the Thames Valley, one by the Hampton Trust in Hampshire and one by the Lucy Faithfull Foundation (LFF) at various locations in England and Wales. In 2005 Quakers and LFF were given funding to continue for another year, and Manchester Community Chaplaincy was also given some statutory funding to begin a Circles project. The Hampshire pilot set up one Circle during its initial three years and has handed over responsibility for work in Hampshire to Quakers. Other initiatives are now emerging around Britain and are seeking advice and support from the Quakers. In addition to running the pilot, Quakers are contributing to the wider promotion of the Circles concept in Britain.

Quakers do not expect to remain deeply involved in either aspect of the work, because the aim has always been to get Circles widely established in Britain and it is confidently expected to outgrow their capacity to run it. The hope is to hand over the work in such a way that it has the best chance of flourishing in the future.

Learning from the pilots

The pilots have proved that there are suitable core members (high risk, high needs sex offenders who want help to avoid reoffending) and enough suitable volunteers. There is an encouraging level of interest among statutory agencies and faith communities.

The Thames Valley pilot has had a number of advantages which have enabled it to set up and maintain a relatively high number of Circles. These have included working in a set geographical area; a history of formal partnerships with police, probation and prisons; better funding and hence more staffing; and staff who were already known and trusted by relevant agencies in the area. There have been many advantages in being an independent body, able to be flexible about individual circumstances and to act as an advocate for offenders when appropriate. Balancing voluntary and statutory involvement remains an essential part of the concept. The future structures need to build on this experience and on other lessons which the evaluation is drawing out.

A new structure

It is planned to set up two new independent charitable companies to provide and co-ordinate Circles – that is, to take over both aspects of the work currently being done by Quakers.

A new body will be needed to take over from Quakers the management of Hampshire and Thames Valley Circles with the capacity to expand carefully so that resources and expertise are not over-stretched. Thames Valley and Hants/Isle of Wight form a whole prisons area (part of the south east regional government area), which fits with the developing structures of the National Offender Management Service (NOMS) (see below). The new body will need a start-up grant from the Home Office but might then depend on a procurement arrangement for provision of Circles management. The present Steering Group, which includes representatives of the four partner bodies, will play an important part in determining the future structure.

It is also seen as important to have an organisation in a position to ensure that all bodies using the name 'Circles of Support and Accountability' in the UK meet certain standards and keep in touch with one another. Some form of membership or affiliation would ensure that all bodies running 'Circles of Support and Accountability' are in formal relationship with one another.

Emerging Circles projects might look to the national body and/or to more experienced regional projects for help, advice and consultancy. Somewhere in the structure there also needs to be the capacity to support and advise bodies such as faith communities which want to set up more informal circles within their own communities. This side of the work might be suitable for fundraising from trusts and individual donors.

The current reorganisation of prisons and probation in England and Wales into the new National Offender Management Service (NOMS) means that it is likely that the present funding arrangements will cease at the end of March 2008. This gives a firm date by which we need to have new structures in place, but it also provides an opportunity to design a Circles structure to fit this new way of working. From 2008, NOMS will be based on the purchaser-provider model, with regions purchasing services such as Circles from organisations offering the service. This should provide a more robust basis for funding than the present grants from the Home Office, enabling staffing levels to respond to demand for Circles. Other potential purchasers of Circles include the Scottish Executive (or Scottish regions) and voluntary bodies such as the churches. Two other possible sources of funding are the police (who are not part of NOMS but are very much part of the Multi-Agency Public Protection Arrangements – MAPPA – with which Circles work closely), and various agencies who might find it useful to pay for us to provide them with training in how to work with sex offenders, either alongside our own volunteers or separately.

National, regional and local levels

We currently envisage a national office, responsible for: promotion of the concept; good practice and minimum standards; membership/affiliation; advice and staff training; setting up new projects; relationships with national bodies, voluntary and statutory;

international contacts; media relations; handbooks, standard protocols, etc; monitoring and data collection.

Each English regional government area and Wales would eventually have one or more Circles providers who would have a direct or indirect contractual relationship with the Regional Offender Manager. The Circles provider could be an accredited but independent body or an existing organisation which takes on Circles as a part of its work. An equivalent arrangement could be made in Scotland and possibly in Northern Ireland (where there is a separate Circles project).

Conclusion

From small beginnings, the idea of Circles of Support and Accountability has grown to be seen as an integral part of a comprehensive approach to rehabilitating and resettling high-risk sex offenders. The partnership between the statutory agencies and voluntary sector has worked to support communities to feel more able to manage those it regarded as the greatest danger to them. Through this process the values of responding to need and respecting the potential in every person have been lived out.

Appendix 2
Ideas for group study

The following questions and ideas should provide those who wish
to use this book for group study with material. They are meant
only as suggestions to ease the study of the book. Group leaders
may well devise other ideas to work with. Groups are encouraged
to develop local Crime and Community Justice structures and to
consider other creative ways to deal with criminals and action
at local level: see also Appendix 3, 'Ideas for practical work'. The
Crime and Community Justice Group at Friends House, 173 Euston
Road, London, NW1 2BJ would be interested in any feedback on the
book and other work in this area.

Chapter 1 *Still searching*

Questions
1. What role do you think prisons have in considering the balance
   between the safety of the community and the care of the
   individual offender?
2. How can the emphasis on punishment in our current criminal
   justice system be understood? Why are we so concerned with
   punishing?
3. Suppose you came home to find that your home had been
   broken into and some damage done to it? How would you feel?
   How would it affect you? What questions would you have? What
   would you need?
4. What would be necessary before serious offenders could be
   more readily held within their own community?

Activities
1. Outline the details of a recent court case from the local paper or
   known to members of the group. Discuss what you think are the
   victim's basic needs? Who can and should provide what? What
   could you as an individual do? What could your faith group do?
   The 'system'? The 'community'?
2. What about the offender in the case? What are his/her basic
   needs? What should happen to them? Who should act? What

could you as an individual do? What could your faith group do?

3. Invite someone from your nearby prison or young offender institution to talk with the group about the nature of custody today.

4. Invite someone from the local Victim Support group to talk about the work being done locally with victims of crime.

Chapter 2 *Why Quakers are interested in criminal justice*

Questions

1. How do you understand the significance of the slogans 'if you want peace, work for justice' and 'question authority'?

2. Do you think that people can change their fundamental behaviour, developed over many years?

3. Do you think the public wants to know more about how criminal justice works? Do you think Quakers and other faith groups are interested in the subject?

4. What are the key characteristics behind the work of the reformers from which we can learn today to direct our efforts?

5. Since the discussion about *Six Friends look at Crime and Punishment*, how would you describe the involvement of faith groups in the development of ideas to do with crime and community justice?

6. If you were designing a prison today, what would be the key components of the architecture and the regime that you would see as contributing to the purpose of the place?

7. Which of the main alternatives to imprisonment should be developed in order to increase the diversion from custody? Decriminalisation? Community-based justice systems? Cautioning processes including restorative conferencing? Fines? Community Service? Probation supervision? Curfew orders? Tagging? Attendance centres? Weekend custody? Any others you can think of?

8. What are the implications of starting a Crime and Community Justice Group in your area, either through groups of Quakers joining with other faith groups or through other interested people? Linking with those currently working in criminal justice through QICJ may provide some ideas.

Activities

1. Invite a local probation officer to discuss the range of community sentence facilities locally and other issues of community justice.
2. Consider having a community-based workshop led by AVP for members of the faith group and others – three days, but a taster can be arranged for a couple of hours.
3. Arrange for a talk from someone from Lifelines or a local Quaker Prison Minister; or find out about Glebe House. Addresses are at the end of Appendix 3.

Chapter 3 *Criminal justice today*

Questions

1. Discuss the five functions of prisons as described on page 35 by Thomas Mathieson. Can you think of examples that support the functions? Can you suggest further functions that prisons fulfil?
2. Consider the objectives of the criminal justice system as outlined on page 37. With this broader perspective, what are the key differences and the likely outcomes from this list of six objectives? Are they more challenging than the previous list, and what are the likely pitfalls in their implementation?
3. What are the significant features of the 'nothing works' climate of the 1960s and 70s and how do they begin to contrast with the optimism of the 'what works' movement of the late 1980s and 90s? What are the risks involved in depending on these ideas for future policy building?
4. Do you think that 'prison works'?
5. Are you concerned about the rise of the prison population? What do you think the causes are, and what are the consequences?
6. What are the alternatives to an increased prison population and how could that be achieved? What resistance would you be likely to meet and how would you consider countering it in order to convince decision-makers and sentencers?
7. Discuss the concepts of rehabilitation, deterrence, incapacitation, and retribution. How valid are they today in our thinking? What alternatives could we consider?

Activity

1. Put together a model of the sort of prison, with its regime, that you could justify.

Chapter 4 *Restorative justice and community safety*

Questions

1. Restorative justice will probably be an attractive concept to most of those reading this book. If so, do you see it as replacing much of traditional criminal justice? Would there be drawbacks to this?
2. From the Canadian experience in 'Restorative Justice in Action' can we discern areas for our exploration given the opportunities and the will?
3. What would you personally worry about if initiatives like the Thames Valley Partnership were in use throughout your area?

Activity

1. Compile a list of issues that you would like to see in your area to make it safer. Follow that with an action plan of how it could be achieved.

Chapter 5 *Restorative and community justice working*

Questions

1. How would you feel if you were asked to meet someone who had stolen something from you?
2. What Quaker wisdom would you want to have in your pocket to remind you of how you would wish to behave? You may wish to look through *Quaker Faith and Practice* for ideas.

Activity

1. Consider the two pieces about the Ludlow Partnership. Members of the group could take roles and play the part of the police, the faith community members, the young people in trouble, those not yet in trouble, the family members on the estate and describe the feelings before the development of the project and after. What would each group want for the future?
2. If there is a partnership like the Ludlow Partnership in your area, try to get someone to talk to the group, or consider whether you can identify a local need for one.

Chapter 6 *Theology, justice and forgiveness*

Questions

1. Which would cause you the greater anxiety – to hear that the

bishop/overseer was calling round to discuss a sin he had heard you had committed, or to hear that the police would be popping in because of suspicions that you had committed a crime? What does this say about our social values? Does the connection between sin and offending mean anything to you?

2. What does repentance and forgiveness mean to you?
3. Is forgiveness compatible with the legal system? Is it an appropriate concern in relation to crime? If so, how can it be encouraged? What dangers do you foresee?
4. What place has anger got in the situation? What can be done with the anger we experience as victims?
5. What is the relationship between guilt and punishment? Does punishment relieve guilt? Should it? What are the alternatives?
6. How can the criminal justice system help with forgiveness and re-integration? In the description of a process on page 81–83 consider the four issues of a possible restorative adjudicating forum. Can you see this working? What would it take to bring it about and to be regularly used?

Activity
1. Examine news clippings of crime coverage from your local paper. List and discuss ways that news coverage of crime encourages fear as well as stereotypes and misconceptions about crime, victims, offenders, officials and the justice process.

Chapter 7 *Quaker Social Testimony*

Questions
1. How can Quaker testimonies provide an approach to crime and community justice that could give us new insights into the way things could be? Equality, Community, Simplicity, Stewardship, Integrity and Truth, Peace and Social Testimonies all have perspectives that could be developed.
2. What are the factors we might consider significant in our path towards spiritual discernment in crime and community justice?
3. What are the major changes we would want to bring about in the way we order our justice system?
4. What is it about crime that makes us view it differently from other wrongs and harms? Should we view and treat it differently? If so, where would you draw the line between them?

Activities
1. Ask the group to take positions on a series of statements. Ask those who wish to disagree to stand at one end of the room, those registering agreement at the other, and those undecided to stand in the centre. They will need to rearrange themselves after each statement. Pause to discuss the reasons for your opinions between each statement.

   Sample statements (make your own):
   – The death penalty should be used for all murderers.
   – The death penalty should be used for the worst murderers only.
   – Spouse abuse should be declared and treated as a crime.
   – People who commit crime should pay for it by going to prison.
   – The hitting of children should be a crime.

2. List the factors from testimonies that may have a bearing on the stance people have taken in the previous activity.

Chapter 8 *Organisational and cultural change*

Questions
1. What is meant by a 'paradigm'?
2. What are some of the paradigms we use in everyday life to understand the world, in family relationships, at work, in sporting activities?
3. Why does the author say that it is particularly difficult to change an organisation or system? How does the paradigm fit into this thinking? Can you think of how paradigms can affect the way we think about problems and solutions?
4. In considering the cultural web, take as an example your own faith group and review each of the six elements that make up the web around the paradigm in relation to your it. *Power structures* (formal and informal, implicit, unspoken), *Organisational structures* (the links between various parts of the faith group), *Control systems* (how are resources and activities managed), Routines and Rituals (protocols, language and procedures taken for granted), *Myths and Stories* (what is celebrated as depicting the essence of the group), *Symbols* (what icons or symbolic activities say something crucial about the group).
5. There are changes described in the way that the criminal justice

paradigm could be considered to be changing – can you think of failures or crises that might bring about further change? What opportunities could there be in the next 20 years?

6. Consider current reforms in criminal justice matters – victim support, electronic monitoring (tagging), private prisons, community service, joined up local agencies (coterminosity). To what extent do they point in new directions? To what extent are reinforcing the past paradigm?

Activity

1. Suppose two children get into a fight at school and one knocks out a tooth from the other. This could be treated as a problem requiring punishment, a conflict needing resolution, or a damage requiring restitution. It could be seen as something to settle within the school or as a criminal case, or it could be taken to a civil court. All these and other responses can and do occur in such situations.

Chapter 9 *Working with the Cultural Change*

Questions

1. Can we recognise the factors which contribute towards social disharmony and which can lead to criminal behaviour? List some of them in a brainstorming exercise. Consider ways in which those factors could be addressed so that the individual does not have to take all the responsibility for the outcome.

2. Consider the Myth of the Scapegoat and look at ways in which the good in offenders is often denied so that we can continue to deal with them in the way we do. How does the media portray serious offenders? What do you feel about the last report you read about a rape or a murder? What was your view about the last report about drug dealing? Can you consider the quote from Solzhenitsyn on page 101 within the context of your own breaking of the law in your own mind, or in reality? Why do we find it so hard to respect the potential in the most damaging?

3. The Myth of Banishment tries to deny that prisoners are coming out in almost as great numbers as they are going into prison. Do we appreciate the dynamics of returning to the community? How can we challenge this myth and celebrate an alternative

one – perhaps of the reformed offender now doing good deeds as a model citizen?

4. The way the Myth of Punishing the Guilty solves the problem leads us to question the separation of innocent from guilty. What part do we play in the conditions which lead to crime ridden areas in our cities and in the unrealistic aspirations we set for many in society without equipping them with the skills or capacities to reach those goals?

Activities

1. Role-play elements from the myths Scapegoat, Banishment and Finality of punishment – particularly taking the roles of the judge describing the words at sentencing, the offender understanding the consequences of the myth, the victim witnessing these processes and wondering where they fit in, and the family of the offender describing the situation to their neighbours.

2. Devise three alternative myths to challenge the three described here and consider ways in which they could be celebrated and promoted in such a way that they become accepted as a myth supporting a preventative paradigm rather than the punishing one in which we currently are caught up.

Chapter 10 *Ideas in action*

Questions

1. Can you find examples in your local media of stories of reconciliation, mediation and understanding?

2. Does Restorative Justice seem common sense to you? Consider the questions at the end of Elizabeth's Story. What are the advantages of the traditional system and the disadvantages? What are the advantages and disadvantages of restorative justice?

3. In considering 'Lorraine's Story' consider the roles of Lorraine, Keith Stanley and review the feelings involved in the process of their meeting. There are phases of anticipation, preparation, commitment, uncertainty, and delivery. What would your view be if asked to arrange such a meeting in future? How could such events be prepared for? Should this process be more readily available to victims and offenders? What protocols would be necessary to enable it to happen more regularly?

Activity

1. Build up a scrap book of positive reactions to conflict and bring it to your friends' and colleagues' attention.

Chapter 11 *Proposals for a way ahead*

Questions

1. Consider the principles described in the first paragraph on page 119 and discuss the implications for your group in working with those ideas. Would you be able to support them all? What are the implications for local action for you? What more may you need in order to understand the implications of the principles? Where could you seek information, support, guidance, partnership etc?

2. What does the slogan 'Tough on Crime, Tough on the Causes of Crime' conjure up for you, rhetoric or opportunity? Use of other phrases such as Tough Justice, Tough Love etc. stem from a need to balance care and control in order to achieve improvements – do you agree on the need for balance?

3. How could we work towards restoring the series of processes in including the offender back into the community – Sin, Guilt, Punishment, Expiation, Reparation, Forgiveness and Reconciliation – so that we do not use the exclusion of prison so much.

4. Could we decriminalise much more anti-social behaviour and encourage that it be dealt with at local level within the civil law process or through community justice processes of mediation and restorative justice?

5. The worldwide nature of the problem leads us to consider the implications on a much wider canvas. The new agenda on page 123 gives us a big range of subjects to be tackled by the agencies seeking reform. How can the group focus on the main issues that may lead to other changes? Is it helpful to have such a wide view of the subject? Should faith groups focus on the local and achievable smaller issues? Is it possible to combine the two in converting faith into action?

Activities

1. In considering the new agenda list the main changes possible within your country and in one other country your group is

aware of. How feasible are the changes and what would it take to achieve them?

2. Does the list of actions being taken at present lead you to think that major change is possible in the future? Which are the three most important of the nine issues listed in that section?

3. Design a programme of reform in your country based on the new agenda and consider the process whereby it can be achieved?

Chapter 12 *Towards a vision of Community Justice*

Questions

1. Can we learn from the Canadian experience of faith communities working with offenders in Circles of Support and Accountability and through Victim Offender Reparation Programmes? What would your group need to become so involved with local offenders when they are released? Do you know how many ex-offenders are living in your locality? What kind of support have they got currently?

2. Are you aware of the work taking place within youth justice procedures in your local authority area? Have you been able to study the crime-prevention strategy for your area? If not, it is suggested that this would provide an excellent activity period of study and discussion. What could you do about involvement in the prevention strategy?

3, Does the communitarian approach towards prison arrangements seem to you helpful in increasing accountability to the local community? Would this lead to greater involvement by people nearby?

4. What deeds could the group consider becoming involved with and be confident of sustaining? Would partnerships with other groups or sharing work within one of the current agencies help this achievement?

5. Have faith groups considered the potential of their networking potential in carrying out a piece of work over an area or locality? What sort of issue do you think might unite groups in working together with some urgency and imagination?

Activities

1. Ask a probation officer to speak to the group about the range of

community based support for those on supervision either on probation, parole or post-custody.

2. Describe the elements of an approach to crime and community justice that is thoroughly restorative? How would it work?

3. Outline the elements that could be implemented now, which might take us towards the direction of restorative justice.

Appendix 3
Ideas for practical work

The Future

Where are the callings for Friends to focus their witness in the future?

- Should Quaker witness be against the increasing privatisation of the criminal justice agencies with the consequential impetus to develop more and more systems and areas for intervention because of the profit motive?
- Does the increased technological surveillance of our lives cause us concern as an intervention in civil liberties?
- The move towards detaining those who are diagnosed as having a severe personality disorder until they are considered to be no longer a risk raises concerns about the infringement of liberty for what people might do rather than what they have done.
- The continuing detention of young people in prison establishments whose size and culture inhibits any real process of change and growth must lead to anxieties about the direction of social policy, when the rehabilitation rates are considered.
- The rise in the number of women in prison has been a concern for the Scottish Prison Service, so much so that in 1998 a commitment was given to halve the population in five years. Although there has not been such a commitment in England and Wales, there remain pressures from Friends and many other groups to reduce the numbers of women in prison. To achieve this it would be necessary to find alternative community-based facilities that could help them gain control in their lives and to develop more women-centred programmes and a range of regimes in prisons. The added damage to society through the custody of women who are primary carers for others adds urgency to the need to seek workable alternatives. Female prisoners account for 6 per cent of the prison population in 2005 (4.5 per cent in 1999 and 3.6 per cent in 1987). The rise in the average population was substantially higher (51 per cent) than the rise in the male population (24 per cent). This rapid change in patterns of offending and sentencing practice continues to be a cause for concern.

- The proportion of ethnic minority prisoners at over 18 per cent of the total number when the national proportion of British population is 6 per cent leads us to examine the institutional racism which has been recognised in most criminal justice agencies. The events following the Stephen Lawrence murder and the report arising from it have brought about policies of change within all agencies and government departments that will need our support over the next few years. The inquiry into the Mubarrak murder in Feltham, however, shows that much remains to be done.
- The rise in alternative approaches to justice has given many working in agencies and organisations experience of restorative justice, a concept that reflects many of the hopes for a more personal and inclusive environment.

Work in hand

- Family issues are being addressed through the process of change after the consultation paper Supporting Families, which proposed better support for parents, strengthening marriage relationships and developing a family and parenting institute supported by a helpline.
- Domestic violence is being addressed through protection measures in the Family Law Act and through the examination of issues under the local crime audit system and the statutory 'community safety plans'. A new awareness campaign, 'Breaking the Chain', was launched.
- The care system is being more closely scrutinised over a three-year programme to improve the delivery of childcare services. 'Quality Protects' was established in 1999, with £375 million over three years dedicated to significant improvements.
- The Sure Start programme continues to support early years' education.
- School exclusions are being tackled through a programme worth £500 million over three years to support pupils and tackle unruly classroom behaviour. The crime reduction programme is also contributing to improve schools' management of attendance, behaviour and bullying.
- Combating drug abuse is being addressed through health and local authorities providing new treatment programmes and a

new prevention advisory service.

- Improvements related to youth offending include halving the time it takes to come to court, working with teams across agencies to focus on addressing the factors contributing to youth offending, and seeking to make early interventions to assist the prevention of further offending.
- Informing the public about offenders and the risks they represent is an important aspect of seeking to reduce the risks and lead to a safer society. Multi-agency Public Protection Panels have achieved greater confidence about managing the risk.
- Victims are provided with support through Victim Support, with the help of government funding and through its witness service schemes developed in courts.

Things you can do – be informed and inform others

- Seek information from national groups and become involved in the debate. There are often local groups allied to the national organisations. Addresses are given at the end of this appendix.
- Become more aware of local issues through contact with the courts, the social services, the police, probation and prison services. Seeking information can often open up areas of need for involvement and support or challenge and change.
- See the present system at work by attending court hearings.
- Then, empowered by facts, lobby MPs, councillors, Home Secretary, Lord Chancellor and so on, more effectively.

Things you can do – support and join existing networks

- Pressure groups such as Howard League, NACRO, Prison Reform Trust, Centre for Criminal Studies – encouraging them to promote restorative justice.
- Mediation UK: a network of projects, organisations and individuals interested in mediation and other constructive forms of conflict resolution. Offers Directory of Services, publication lists, information about conferences and training events. Has special interest networks in Community Mediation and Victim/Offender Mediation.
- AVP Britain: In AVP workshops prisoners and community members are encouraged to use their skills of open-minded

listening to the other party, clearly communicating their own needs, and negotiating agreements through which both parties gain something and harmony is maintained. Offers workshops, training, newsletter.

- Quakers in Criminal Justice (QICJ): a network of members of the Religious Society of Friends involved in the criminal justice system.
- Restorative Justice Consortium: an umbrella organisation producing standards for practice, bringing together interested parties and working hard to represent restorative values within the justice system.
- Transforming Conflict: working to develop restorative justice in education with training, workshops and whole school approaches.

Things you can do – learn techniques

- Learn and practice non-punitive responses/conflict resolution/mediation.
- Schools work – peer mediation/conflict resolution/no blame approach.
- AVP Workshops – first and second level, training for facilitators.
- Restorative Justice facilitation.

Things you can do – promote restorative justice

- Through service as a prison visitor – to befriend individual prisoners who request the relationship through a chaplain or another member of staff of your local prison.
- Through service as a prison volunteer – helping to 'break down' the walls through various activities:
  - visits – as family supporters
  - crèches – assist childcare during visits
  - tutors with particular skills – assisting educational classes
  - sports enthusiasts – sharing experience and expertise/ arranging fixtures with outside groups
  - discussion groups – through the chaplaincy or education department
  - preparation for release groups – particularly helping with employment interview skills and problem-solving approaches
  - attending religious services in the prison – through the

chaplaincy and joining the prayer support group which often exists attached to the prison. Using the prayer sheet produced by the chaplain can be a start into a greater awareness of the complexity of need.

- Probation Voluntary Associates – via local Chief Probation Officer.
- Victim Support or Court Witness volunteers.
- Magistrate – you can be proposed by your Monthly Meeting, a Trade Union or other organisation or offer yourself as an individual.
- Advocates, befrienders or similar – inquire through the Chief Constable whether the local police station uses such volunteers.
- Become a member of a MM penal affairs or QPM support group
- Become a volunteer with your local community or victim/offender mediation service.
- Join a circle of support and accountability if they are present locally.
- Run a conference on restorative justice/conflict resolution/mediation.
- Form a discussion group.
- Whatever your profession, look round to see where mediation would be fruitful.

Some useful addresses

- Secretary of the Crime and Community Justice Group, Friends House, Euston Road, London NW1 2BJ
  020 7663 1000

- Secretary of the Crime and Community Justice Group, Quaker Peace & Social Witness, Friends House, 173 Euston Road, London NW1 2BJ
  020 7663 1000

- Alternatives to Violence Project
  0845 458 2692
  www.avpbritain.org.uk

- Glebe House: specialist work with teenage males with sexual issues
  Friends Therapeutic Community Trust, Shudy Camps,

Cambridgeshire CB1 6RB
01799 584 359
info@glebehouse.org.uk

- Howard League for Penal Reform
  1 Ardleigh Road, London N1 4HS
  020 7249 7373
  www.howardleague.org

- James Nayler Foundation: dedicated to understanding and
  treating personality disorders
  Unit B6, Spithead Industrial Estate, Shanklin, PO33 9PH
  01983 401 700

- Justice
  59 Carter Lane, London EC4V 5AQ
  020 7329 5100
  www.justice.org.uk

- LEAP Confronting Conflict
  8 Lennox Road, Finsbury Park, London N4 3NW
  020 7272 5630
  www.leaplinx.com

- London Mennonite Centre
  14 Shepherds Hill, London N6 5AQ
  020 8340 8775

- Mediation UK
  Alexander House, Telephone Avenue, Bristol BS1 4BS
  0117 904 6661
  www.mediationuk.org.uk

- NACRO (National Association for the Care and Resettlement of
  Offenders)
  169 Clapham Road, London SW9 0PU
  020 7582 6500
  www.nacro.org.uk

- New Bridge
  27A Medway Street, London SW1P 2BD
  020 7976 0779
  www.newbridgefoundation.org.uk

- Prison Service
  To write to HM Prison Service, the address is:
  Parliamentary, Correspondence and Briefing Unit, HM Prison Service HQ, Cleland House, Page Street, London, SW1P 4LN
  www.hmprisonservice.gov.uk

- Quakers in Criminal Justice (QICJ)
  Ann Jacob, Co-Clerk, 83 Drayton Avenue, London W13 0LE
  020 8991 0158
  annj83@googlemail.com

- Restorative Justice Consortium
  Suite 50, Albert Buildings, 49 Queen Victoria Street, London
  EC4N 4SA
  0207 653 1992
  www.restorativejustice.org.uk

- Transforming Conflict: The National Centre for Restorative Justice in Education
  Mortimer Hill, Mortimer, Berkshire RG7 3PW
  0118 933 1520

- Victim/Offender Unit
  The Basement, Oxford Place, Leeds, West Yorkshire LS1 3AX
  0113 2435932

- Victim Support – National Office
  Cranmer House, 39 Brixton Road, London SW9 6DZ
  020 7735 9166
  www.victimsupport.org.uk

Key issues in the development of prisons in England and Wales to 2005

Year	Event	Prison Pop'n
11th cent.	Anglo-Saxon Chronicle records that William the Conqueror 'caused castles to be built which were a great burden to the poor' and they put people in the dungeons or oubliettes.	
17th cent.	The use of imprisonment for reformation, work and religious instruction was developing in Holland and Germany.	
18th cent.	Until the War of Independence convicts were transported to North American and Caribbean colonies on conditional pardon.	
1777	John Howard published *The State of the Prisons in England and Wales*. This showed a lack of any effective and accountable system of administration. Reformers Romilley, Bentham, Fowell Buxton and Elizabeth Fry followed.	
1820	Transportation to New South Wales and Van Diemen's Land (Tasmania).	
1821	Millbank Prison built on the site of what is now the Tate Gallery and was under the responsibility of the Home Secretary to house those about to be transported.	
1822	Gaol Act. Robert Peel as Home Secretary established the administration and standards in the county gaols.	
1835	Four Inspectors appointed by the Home Secretary. Start of Prison Rules.	
1842	Pentonville built as a model prison. Period of rapid prison building commenced.	
1843	Home Secretary appointed a Surveyor-General to advise on prison building.	
1848	Edwin Chadwick Report on prisons showed that they reflected the poor social conditions generally prevalent in society.	
1849	Prisons Act. The Director of Convict Prisons assumed responsibility for 50 prisons. Administration framework	

in place, but it was still the era of solitary confinement, the treadmill and crank.

1865 Prisons Act consolidated the position of local prisons and convict prisons. Regimes based on 'hard work, a hard bed and hard fare' introduced.

1866 Transportation discontinued. Hulks used to hold those awaiting transportation continued in use for some decades.

1877 Prisons Act marked the level of demolition and rebuilding taking place. Era of inspectors – a considerable legacy of Victorian times. Centralisation of control, funding transferred from local to central funds.

1878 The management of the prison system was vested in the Home Secretary, delegated to the Prison Commissioners. 113 county, borough and liberty prisons formerly supervised by the justices became the responsibility of the Commission.Commissioners collected information about 113 prisons and closed 38 owing to an excess of places. Establishment of standardised administration, controlled resources, improved basic conditions. The silent system, hard labour and separation remained in the penitentiaries.'A massive machine for the promotion of misery'. Some moderation of punishments. No more wearing of masks outside cells and no more flogging in front of assembled prisoners.   20,000

1888 Reduction of crime rates but continued criticism of prison regimes

1894 led to the establishment of the Gladstone Committee of Enquiry.

1895 Gladstone Report – ideas of centralised organisation, indictment of past treatment regimes, separate accommodation and separation of groups, treadmill and crank abandoned, remission and industrial training introduced, books introduced for selected prisoners; talking permitted for the well-behaved ones. Aftercare concept developed with a Prisoners Aid Society, a medical member of the Board, annual conferences of staff commenced to raise standards and awareness.

1898	Prison Act. The Home Secretary introduced the classification of prisoners but inspection was not independent.	18,500
1899	Young offenders began to be separately trained in Borstal, Rochester.	
1903		20,000
1904	Borstal system introduced.	
1908	Borstals Authorised and Preventive Detention introduced as a sentence owing to the concerns about the increase of recidivism. Half of the prison population in for non-payment of fines. Alternative sentences developed. Winston Churchill, Home Secretary.	22,000
1914	Release of many prisoners.	18,000
1915	Establishment of Prison Officers Representative Board, start of union representation.	
1918	Decriminalisation of drunkenness.	9,000
1919	Strike by prison officers, 74 dismissed. Abolition of the term 'warder', replaced by 'officer'.	
1922	Development of borstals maintained, education introduced; the arrow mark on the uniform abandoned, prison crop abolished, physical education introduced and the rules of silence relaxed – 'idle gossip not intended'. First conference of Governors, which became an annual event. Prison Officers Association established.	11,000
1932	Dartmoor Riot.	
1938	Prison Officers Association recognised formally.	11,000
1939	Half the prison population discharged. Staff College opened to train prison officers.	5,750
1940		8,850
1942		12,000
1945	Staff of 3,300 of all grades.	15,000
1948	Criminal Justice Act abolished penal servitude, hard labour and the division of offenders by sentence.	
1949	Framework of Statutory Rules established to regulate the organisation. Rule 1: 'The purpose of the training and treatment of convicted prisoners shall be to encourage and assist them to lead a good and useful	

	life.' Hostel in Bristol introduced for preventative detention prisoners.	
1950	Borstal success maintained, Detention Centres started.	20,400
1951	Two thousand men serving preventive detention.	
1952		24,000
1953	Advisory Council on the Treatment of Offenders recommended the abolition of preventive detention.	
1954	Disturbances in Parkhurst and Wandsworth.	
1955	United Nations Minimum Rules approved. The era known as the 'golden years' followed in which concepts of dignity, self-respect and humanity were given formal and lasting expression.	20,400
1956	Prison welfare officers appointed. Seven thousand staff in all.	20,000
1957	Staff College course to train Assistant Governors.	
1961	Criminal Justice Act abolished the Prison Commission, with responsibility transferred to the Home Office. Owing to the rise in numbers to three in a cell, a major building programme commenced. 'The evil of overcrowding seems now to be accepted as inevitable, even by prisoners.'	30,000
1962	Group work schemes developed. Hostels for pre-release population growing.	
1963	Abolition of death penalty. Development of longer sentences, introduction of parole.	30,000
1964	Escape of train robbers led to a crisis of confidence in security.	
1965	Escape of George Blake from Wormwood Scrubs. Mountbatten Enquiry focused upon security of physical structures, systems of management and the location of prisoners. A switch of priorities followed which symbolically changed the Service with the introduction of electronics, secure perimeters, dogs and control rooms. Recommended concentration of high risk prisoners not followed, but following the Advisory Council on the Penal System the dispersal of such risks was commenced with the building of new high security prisons.	34,000

1969	8,500 prisoners were sharing cells designed for one person. Parkhurst Riot.	35,000
1970	In twenty years the prison population had doubled.	40,000
1972	Several disturbances and demonstrations in prisons. Gartree Riot the most serious. Industrial relations difficulties developed.	
1975	15,600 prisoners sharing accommodation.	40,800
1976	Hull Riot, a serious internal breakdown. Leicester escape, a serious external breakdown. Changes in management resulted. Concept of neighbourhood borstal developed with success.	42,000
1979	May Committee established to consider Industrial Relations. Concept of humane containment in force. General Election – Conservative victory.	42,220
1980		42,264
1981	Financial Management Initiative developing. Industrial relations difficulties experienced.	43,311
1982	Criminal Justice Act 1982 – short, sharp, shock sentences in Detention Centres and the abolition of 'Borstal Training'.	43,707
1983	Prison disturbances in Wormwood Scrubs and Albany. Major changes in parole system. General election – Conservative victory	43,462
1984	Introduction of Circular Instruction 55/84 which began business planning systems in prisons.	43,925
1985	Industrial relations tensions. Series of prison riots.	46,238
1986	Harsher sentences for drug offenders.	46,889
1987	Fresh Start initiative in Prison Service – abolition of overtime. General election – Conservative victory	48,963
1988	Criminal Justice Act 1988 – harsher sentences for serious offences. Introduction of Prison Service Statement of Purpose.	49,949
1989	Introduction of telephones on prison wings.	48,610
1990	Serious prison disturbances throughout the summer beginning with Strangeways.	45,817
1991	Woolf Report into prison disturbances 1990 published Criminal Justice Act 1991 – 'just deserts' ideology.	45,897

	Prisons Ombudsman introduced. Board of Visitors' disciplinary role ended.	
1992	Prison Security Act – defined new offence of prison mutiny and assisting escape. Routine censoring of all prisoners' mail ends. April – HMP The Wolds, the first privately run prison, opens. The Lygo Report on prison management recommends agency status.	45,817
1992	General Election – Conservative victory.	
1993	Murder of James Bulger. Criminal Justice Act 1993. Michael Howard appointed Home Secretary – 'Prison Works' speech. Prison Service became an executive agency under the leadership of Derek Lewis. Riot at Wymott Prison. First market-tested prison – Strangeways awarded to the public sector.	44,566
1994	Criminal Justice and Public Order Act 1994 – increased sentence provision for juvenile offenders. Creation of two thousand prison places. First Service Level Agreement signed for Strangeways Prison. Escape of armed prisoners from Special Security Unit at Whitemoor Prison in September. Woodcock Report into escape published in December.	48,794
1995	Escape of three lifers from HMP Parkhurst. Learmont Report into escape published in September. 'Three Strikes' policy proposed at Conservative Party Conference. Introduction of Mandatory Drug Testing and Incentives and Earned Privileges Scheme across Prison Service. Richard Tilt replaces the sacked Derek Lewis as Director General – the first former governor to hold the post. Introduction of 'boot-camp'-style regimes for young offenders. Prison overcrowding leads to the purchase of the prison ship.	51,047
1996	'Slopping out' ended with the completion of installation of integral sanitation in all prisons. Introduction of Sex Offender Treatment Programme – first accredited offending behaviour programme.	55,281
1997	Crime Sentences Act 1997 – mandatory sentences introduced under two or three strikes policy. Disturbance at Full Sutton Prison. General election – Labour victory.	61,114

1998	Crime and Disorder Act 1998 – concentrating on juvenile crime and the youth justice system – also the full abolition of capital punishment. Disturbance at Full Sutton Prison. Launch of major enquiry into allegations of abuse at Wormwood Scrubs.	65,298
1999	Report into the murder of Stephen Lawrence. Changes in the youth justice system leads to the creation of the Youth Justice Board and plans for separate juvenile prisons. Martin Narey replaces Sir Richard Tilt as Director General. Substantial (£226 million) additional funding (via CSR) allocated to develop drug strategy and regime programmes.	65,586
2000	Performance Management culture strengthened by Martin Narey with an emphasis on the decency culture and a robust approach to delivery and poor performance. Race relations issues take greater emphasis. Wormwood Scrubs inquiry into serious allegations of staff violence in the Segregation Unit.	64,816
2001	Notions of citizenship, decency and respect being 64,576 worked upon. Private prisons continue to grow in numbers but through testing processes the Service takes back a privately run prison – Blakenhurst 2002 Publication of the Social Exclusion Unit's Report *Reducing Re-offending by Ex-Prisoners*	67,474
2003	Martin Narey becomes Commissioner of Correctional Services and Phil Wheatley Director General of the Prison Service. Closer working between prisons and Probation Services signalled. Riot at Lincoln Prison.	71,498
2004	Establishment of the National Offender Management Service following consultation about the Carter Report on corrections work.	74,000
2005	NOMS developed till the election. Martin Narey resigns to work with Barnardos.	78,000
2007		80,000

Glossary of terms

Anti-social personality disorder – through formative experiences it is known that personalities can develop in dysfunctional ways so that later behaviour can be disturbing and dangerous. The possibility of changing the behaviour of those with anti-social personality disorder is still being researched, but there is little evidence for success (apart from a few programmes and the therapeutic community approach). The main emphasis is consequently focused upon managing the setting for such people through the boundaries established in prison and other supervisory settings.

Circles of Support and Accountability – a concept originating in Ontario in 1994, where it was recognised that sex offenders were released without support or supervision, and communities felt powerless when these prisoners were released. See Appendix 1.

Classification of prisoners – separating those on remand from the convicted, the young from the old and the male from the female, in order to provide for greater safety of individuals and groups. In England and Wales, adult male prisoners are also categorised by the risk of escape they are presumed to present and then held in prisons of suitable security levels.

Community justice – the concept promoted by Mike Nellis during his Rowntree Fellowship. He linked community safety, restorative justice and hostility to custody in promoting a more locally responsive and involved approach to justice. The formation of local Crime and Community Justice Groups has taken this work further.

Communicative theory of punishment – this proposes that the purpose of punishment is to communicate to citizens that anti-social behaviour is unacceptable. There are consequences arising from such acts showing that the concern to ensure behaviour is maintained within certain boundaries to maintain community safety. Sanctions are applied to persons who commit such acts to mark boundaries of acceptable behaviour and to promote community safety. To make this approach work effectively there is a strong need to report the decisions of sanctions to the public in order to raise awareness.

Communitarian system – the emphasis is on the collective aspects of society, on expressing and developing shared values and commitments, rather than focusing on the individual's rights.

Comprehensive Spending Review – the process whereby the British government reviewed its spending priorities in 1997, the first year in office, and then determined allocation on the basis of achieving the delivery of key outcomes in priority areas of policy. Thus strategic priorities of education, health and tackling drugs were funded action areas. Within the criminal justice system the emphasis has been upon resolving the issues concerned with youth justice and a focus upon evidence-based effective programmes.

Consequentialist view of punishment – the view that criminal acts have automatic consequences and that these should be well understood and with little discretion within the disposal of the punishment.

Criminal justice system – the concept that all the statutory agencies (the courts, Police, Crown Prosecution Service, Probation and Prisons) working within criminal justice can be considered to be a system. In reality there is little system but more a process with many local variations.

Dangerousness – there has been much debate about the state of dangerousness in seeking to understand and treat the condition. The current approach is to consider dangerousness through a process of rigorous risk assessment about the likelihood of repeated behaviour which will threaten others' safety. The process involves a range of reports and actuarial factors such as past behaviour and factors that predispose towards anti-social conduct.

Deterrence – the effect a particular sentence is thought to have upon the behaviour of the individual offender in helping to stop future misbehaviour through the fear of the consequences. Deterrence is also thought to have a general effect in that the example of punishment on offenders is considered to have an effect on the general community as others see what happened to the offender and are inhibited from following the example.

Evidence-based practice – with the development of research into social sciences it is possible to identify those programmes and protocols that are more likely to be successful in achieving the outcome desired from a particular policy. The current government has placed an emphasis upon such practice in determining policies for the integration of various departmental approaches to an issue. Thus, in the area of addressing offending behaviour, the research shows that targeted courses on selected groups of offenders, when carried out within certain disciplines of delivery, can have a significant effect upon the reconviction rates of that group. Thus the Sex Offender Treatment Programme is having an effect upon reconviction rates for a group of offenders who in the past were often thought to have little prospect of rehabilitation.

Exclusion/inclusion – The exclusive view of society and citizenship emphasises personal freedom and individual responsibility. A deserving majority who are seen as self-reliant and law-abiding is contrasted with an undeserving, feckless, welfare-dependent and potentially criminal minority. The benefits of citizenship or membership of the community are confined to those who conform to accepted standards or who can afford to pay for them. Human behaviour is thought to be motivated mainly by a desire for material gain or by fear of punishment or disgrace. Such a society is likely to be unsure of itself, suspicious of strangers, hostile to foreigners. It will adopt such measures as the carrying of identity cards, the maintenance of personal records with access to them by those in authority, and the reporting of suspicious persons or events. The inclusive view of society is epitomised by a recognition that the individual has the capacity and will to change. It emphasises respect for human dignity and personal identity, a sense of public duty and social responsibility. It looks towards putting things right for the future rather than seeking to blame and award punishment. Citizenship and membership of the community are permanent features; the duty to conform to the community's standards is matched by an obligation for the community to support its vulnerable and disadvantaged members. Inclusion is seen in a society that is open and compassionate and has some confidence in the future.

Financial Management Initiative – During the 1980s the British government developed an approach towards its departmental effectiveness by introducing private-sector practices and procedures in order to introduce the three e's (economy, efficiency and effectiveness) to public delivery of services. This involved the development of greater financial awareness within departments, the introduction of budgets linked to performance plans and the start of longer-term planning within each area of activity. The skills of civil servants began to move towards managerial priorities and practices. High-trust/low-trust approaches – a high-trust approach within an organisation will be characterised by a flat organisational structure or a matrix structure in which staff will be encouraged to use initiative and take risks in achieving results. There will be little managerial direct supervision and an emphasis upon achieving the end rather than a control of the process whereby the end is achieved. Low-trust approaches are closely controlled in the detail of procedures and protocols; there will be a hierarchical management structure with the capacity for command situations and little discretion afforded to the majority of staff.

Incapacitation – the concept that if we lock up numbers of offenders they will not be able to commit offences and that eventually there will be a reduction in the crime rate. The view is epitomised by Michael Howard, the Home Secretary's 'prison works' speech at the 1993 Conservative Party Conference. The evidence is that in order to achieve a 1 per cent decrease in the level of a particular crime (burglary) the number of offenders jailed would have to increase by 25 per cent (Tarling).

Just deserts – the view developed following concern about the ineffectiveness of treatment programmes in prison revealed through the research in the 1970s (nothing works) and a consequent attack on parole systems. As a result it was proposed by some politicians and criminologists that the basis for sentencing had legitimacy only through the idea of desert – that a particular crime deserved to receive a certain tariff of punishment. This was hoped to limit the use of prison sentences allegedly to improve the offender, but had the opposite effect in a disastrous way. The overcrowding effect in prisons particularly in the United States led to the rapid increase in prison building and the allocation of funding to 'corrections', the title given to community and custodial disposals, which in some states matched that allocated to education.

Listeners – in the 1980s the increase of suicides in prisons led to the development of a partnership with the Samaritans working with prison staff to produce procedures and protocols to reduce the risk of suicide. The introduction of prisoners as Listeners (surrogate Samaritans) was tried in several prisons and is now encouraged in all prisons as a core part of effective support for those who are feeling alienated.

Mandatory sentences – certain sentences have to be passed by judges in certain circumstances: a life sentence for murder, and increasingly certain lengths of sentence for repeat offences such as burglary and violence against the person ('three strikes and you're out').

NGO – Non-Governmental Organisation. Increasingly important in the partnership approach towards the delivery of policy are the links made within the criminal justice process between statutory departments and the number of themed organisations which are concerned with the work in those areas.

New agenda – the range of areas for attention developed through the work of the International Centre for Penal Studies following extensive consultations across countries and cultures.

New Public Management – in the 1980's and 1990's the public sector developed practices of the private sector in an increasing emphasis upon efficiency, effectiveness and above all economy. Thus contracting out public sector work to the private sector became an increasing practice, as well as the introduction of business plans, contracts and performance indicators.

Panopticon – the design of prisons would have been revolutionised if the panopticon had been built in any numbers. It was based on Jeremy Bentham's concept of staff being able to see and control all movement within the prison by having the cell placed in a circle with control from the centre. Only a few were built, and they were expensive and impractical. The idea of constant supervision by staff remains an important theme in the design of prisons, which have focused on a radial design, with cells arranged in wings radiating from the centre, like the spokes of a wheel.

Paradigm – the mindset behind a policy or system, the set of expectations and systems which support a particular approach towards the subject.

Preventive detention – a sentence developed in England to reflect the wish to deter recidivism. If offenders reconvicted persistently, they received a very long sentence (fifteen years or so) to reflect the continued danger to the public they represented. Inadequate offenders tended to receive this type of sentence, which soon fell into disrepute, with concern about its unfairness.

Restorative justice – although the ideas have been around for a long time they have only lately come into a more general consciousness through their application in addressing young offenders' behaviour through group conferencing. The concept is based on considering the needs and responsibilities of offender, victim and community in seeking to resolve the effect of criminal activity. The process of open communication and consent makes the system quite different from the more traditional approach.

Retributivist – the view that a crime deserves a form of punishment in order to meet the need for retribution, paying back by pain for the pain caused to the community and victims.

Reviewable sentences – these are indeterminate sentences that in effect can prevail for the life of the person, stretching over periods of release into the community. They are reviewed by a judicial tribunal, which includes experts and independent representatives.

Struggle for Justice – the title of the text published in 1972 which focused opposition to the passing of sentences designed to rehabilitate the offender (with little evidence).

Technological surveillance – there is increasing use of CCTV in public and private settings to assist with the management of risk to property and people. Alarm systems have proliferated in 1990s. Other technologies such as tagging are in their early days of implementation but there seems little opposition to the continued use of machines in aid of crime reduction.

Therapeutic community – the development of treatment of patients recovering from the Second World War led to the idea and practice that the participation and involvement of members of the ward community in the process of healing, through the development of an experience of supportive community, could have dramatic improving effects. The acceptance of certain key concepts to support the work became the defining feature of therapeutic communities – concepts of democracy, voluntarism, egalitarianism, communitarianism and reality confrontation.

Victim (primary) – the person directly affected by the crime perpetrated upon them or their property.

Victim (secondary) – those associated with the primary victim as family, neighbours, community or similar groups. It is increasingly important to recognise the rippling effects of a crime that can influence many more people than those directly involved.

What Works – through meta-analysis, the technique of clustering many pieces of research together and analysing the results, turned the tide from 'nothing works' in the 1970s and 1980s to 'What Works' in the 90s. The method puts together small and on their own irrelevant statistics in a big 'pool'. The collected data can then be evaluated as a whole. The results show that when work is focused, targeted, disciplined, evaluated and maintained at a high standard there can be a significant treatment effect in reducing recidivism rates (10-15 per cent). What Works programmes include the Sex Offenders Treatment Programme, Reasoning and Rehabilitation, Extended Thinking Skills, and others now developing. The hope engendered through this approach is tempered by an awareness about how complex and long-term the work has to be to address deep-seated criminogenic factors. The programme has been shown to work more effectively when carried out within the community in which the person is going to continue.

Woolf Committees – following the Strangeways riot the report of Lord Woolf into the disturbances in prisons recommended that the criminal justice agencies should work more closely together in order to appreciate the impact that the work of one agency has on the others. Particularly significant is the position of the Prison Service, which is at the end of the line of decisions made by all the other agencies. A Criminal Justice Co-ordinating Committee was established as a national body and a series of local committees were also set up, chaired by judges and now known as Woolf Committees, soon to be called Criminal Justice Strategy Committees. They are currently referred to as Local Criminal Justice Management Boards and have a more managerial role in relation to local targets for key aspects of justice delivery. They are not chaired by judges.

Youth Justice Board – under recent legislation the development of youth justice, which was an electoral priority of the government, has been placed in the hands of an appointed body representing a wide range of statutory and other interests. The Board is developing strategy for the treatment and care of young people in trouble. In particular it will be the purchasing body for custodial services for those under eighteen sentenced by the courts, and as such will have considerable influence in determining the quality of care and treatment programmes developed in young offender settings.

Youth Justice Teams – in each local authority area there is a team established to develop a programme of treatment and care for those young people who are in trouble or at the risk of trouble. The multi-agency approach of the teams will lead to a greater deployment of resources to address the behaviour of young people much earlier in their period of offending.

Reading I have found helpful

American Friends Service Committee (1977): *Struggle for Justice: A Report on Crime and Punishing in America*. Hill and Wang, New York

Bean, P. (1981): *Punishment*. Martin Robertson, Oxford

Beckford, J.A. & Gilliat, S. (1998): *Religion in Prison – Equal Rites in a Multi-Faith Society*. Cambridge University Press, Cambridge

Braithwaite, J. (1989): *Crime, Shame and Reintegration*. Cambridge University Press, Cambridge

Brody, S. (1975): *The Effectiveness of Sentencing*. Home Office Research Study No. 35. HMSO, London

Burnside, J and Baker, N. (1994): *Relational Justice: Repairing the Breach*. Waterside Press, Winchester

Carey, G. (1996): *Restoring Relationships: The Purpose of Prisons*. Prison Reform Trust, London

Cavadino, M. Crow, I. & Dignan, J. (1999): *Criminal Justice 2000: Strategies for a new century*. Waterside Press, Winchester

Cavadino, M. & Dignan, J. (1992): *The Penal System: An Introduction*. Sage, London

Circles of Support and Accountability in the Thames Valley: The First Three Years April 2002 to March 2005. (2005) Quaker Peace & Social Witness, London

Dale, J. (1996): *Beyond the Spirit of the Age*. 1996 Swarthmore Lecture. QHS, London

Devlin, A. (1995): *Criminal Classes: Offenders at School*. Waterside Press, Winchester

Duckett, T.S. (2003): *Surviving Violent Crime – and the Criminal Injuries Compensation Authority*. Witherbys, London

Dunbar, I. & Langdon, A. (1998): *Tough Justice – Sentencing and Penal Policies in the 1990s*. Blackstone Press, London

Edgar, K., O'Donnell, I & Martin, C. (2003): *Prison Violence: the dynamics of conflict, fear and power*. Willan publishing, Cullompton

Edgar, K. & Newell, T. (2006): *Restorative Justice in Prisons: A Guide to Making it Happen*. Waterside Press, Winchester.

Faulkner, D. (1996): *Darkness and Light: Justice, Crime and Management for Today*. Howard League, London

Field, S. (1990): *Trends in Crime and their Interpretation: A Study of Post-war Crime in England and Wales*. Home Office Research Study No. 119. HMSO, London

Foucault, M (1977): *Discipline and Punish. The Birth of the Prison*. Allen Lane, London

Gibson, B. and Cavadino, P. (1995): *Criminal Justice Process*. Waterside Press, Winchester

Goffman, E. (1961): *Asylums: Essays on the Social Situation of Mental Patients and other Inmates*. Anchor Books, New York

Goleman, E. (1995): *Emotional Intelligence: Why It Can Matter More Than IQ*. Bloomsbury, London

Graef, R. (1992): *Living Dangerously: Young Offenders in their Own Words*. Harper Collins, London

Gulliver, P.H. (1963): *Social Control in an African Society – A Study of the Arusha: Agricultural Masai of Northern Tanganyika*. Routledge and Kegan Paul, London

Hadley, M.L. (ed.) (2001): *The Spiritual Roots of Restorative Justice*. State University of New York

Harding, J. (1982): *Victims and Offenders*. National Council for Voluntary Organisations, Occasional Paper Two. Bedford Square Press, London

Home Office (1991): *Prison Disturbances in April 1990: Report of an Inquiry by the Rt. Hon Lord Justice Woolf and His Honour Judge Stephen Tumim*, Cm. 1456. HMSO, London

Home Office (1991): *Custody, Care and Justice: The Way Ahead for the Prison Service in England and Wales*. Cm. 1647. HMSO, London

Home Office (1996): *Protecting the Public: The Government's Strategy on Crime in England and Wales*. Cm. 3190. HMSO, London

Howard,J. (1777): *The State of the Prisons in England and Wales*. Warrington; republished: Montclair, NJ 1973

Lampen, J. (1987): *Mending Hurts*. 1987 Swarthmore Lecture. QHS, London

Lord Woolf and Judge Stephen Tumim (1991): *Prison Disturbances April 1990*. Cm 1456. HMSO, London

Liebling, A (2004): *Prisons and their moral performance: a study of values, quality, and prison life*. Oxford University Press

Liebling, A. & Maruna, S. (ed.) (2005): *The Effects of Imprisonment*. Willan Publishing, Cullompton

Liebmann, M. (ed.): (1998): *Community and Neighbour Mediation.* Cavendish Publishing Ltd, London

Matthews, R. (1999): *Doing Time, An Introduction to the Sociology of Imprisonment.* Macmillan Press Ltd, Basingstoke

Martinson, R. (1974): *What Works? – Questions and Answers about Prison Reform.* The Public Interest, 35: 22–54

Mathieson T. (1965): *Defences of the Weak: A Sociological Study of a Norwegian Correctional Institution.* Tavistock, London

May J. (1979): *Committee of Inquiry into the United Kingdom Prison Services: Report.* Cm 7673. HMSO, London

McGuire, J. (ed.) (1995): *What Works: Research and Practice on the Reduction of Re-offending.* John Wiley and Sons, Chichester

McGuire, J. & Priestley, P. (1985): *Offending Behaviour: Skills and Stratagems for Going Straight.* Batsford Academic, London

Ministry of Justice, New Zealand (1995): *Restorative Justice: A Discussion Paper.* Ministry of Justice, Wellington

Moreland, L. (2001): *An Ordinary Murder.* Aurum Press, London

Nickalls, J. (1975): *George Fox's Journal.* Society of Friends, London

Nicholls, C. (1997): '*Problem-solving Justice*'. Paper given at ISTD Conference 'Repairing the Damage: Restorative Justice in Action', Bristol, 20 March 1997

Partington, M. (2004): *Salvaging the Sacred: Lucy, my sister.* Quaker Books, London

Pilling, J. (1992): 'Back to Basics: Relationships in the Prison Service', in *Perspectives on Prison: A Collection of Views on Prison Life and Running Prisons.* Cm. 2087. HMSO, London

Quill, D. and Wynne, J. (1993): *Victim and Offender Mediation Handbook.* Save the Children, London

Rose, David (1996): *In the Name of the Law: The Collapse of Criminal Justice.* Jonathan Cape, London

Rose, Melvyn (1997): *Transforming Hate to Love: An Outcome Study of the Peper Harow Treatment Process for Adolescents.* Routledge, London

Rutherford, A. (1994): *Criminal Justice and the Pursuit of Decency.* Waterside Press, Winchester

Rutherford, A. (1996): *Transforming Criminal Policy.* Waterside Press, Winchester

Six Quakers look at Crime and Punishment, (1979). QHS, London

Stern, V. (1998): *A Sin Against the Future: Imprisonment in the World*. Penguin, London

Steven, H. (2005): *No Extraordinary Power: Prayer, Stillness and Activism*. Quaker Books, London.

Stockdale, E. and Casale, S. (eds) (1992): *Criminal Justice Under Stress*. Blackstone, London

Tam, H. (ed.) (1996): *Punishment, Excuses and Moral Development*. Avebury, Aldershot

Tarling, R. (1993): *Analysing Offending: Data Models and Interpretations*. HMSO, London

Volf, M. (1996): *Exclusion and Embrace: A Theological Exploration of Identity, Otherness and Reconciliation*. Abingdon Press, New York

Wood, C. (1991): *The End of Punishment: Christian Perspectives on the Crisis in Criminal Justice*. Published on behalf of the Centre for Theology and Public Issues, University of Edinburgh, by Saint Andrew Press, Edinburgh

Wright, M. (1996): *Justice for Victims and Offenders – A Restorative Response to Crime*. Waterside Press, Winchester

Wright, M. (1999): *Restoring Respect for Justice: A Symposium*. Waterside Press, Winchester

Zehr, H. (1990): *Changing Lenses: A New Focus for Crime and Justice*. Herald Press, Scottdale, USA

Zehr, H. (2002): *The Little Book of Restorative Justice*. Good Books, Intercourse, PA

Printed in the United Kingdom
by Lightning Source UK Ltd.
122798UK00001B/481-510/A